"This is a wonderful, highly readable c[...]t
works of the twentieth century. Chris[...]e
the best of our modern heritage."
—Cha[...]es

"Some books about books are a bore, but not this one. It [...]ve
Christian reading during the past century with a sure touch, and since the
pulse of any community is its reading habits, it gives an enlightening overview
of where evangelicals have been going and what they have been doing all this
time. It is a book that was well worth writing—and is well worth reading."
—James Packer, professor, Regent College

"If you enjoy reading books, studying history, learning about writers, and
analyzing the impact of ideas on our world, then this book is for you. You
don't have to agree with all the selections or interpretations to benefit from
these pages. I thought I knew a lot about books and writers, but reading
this book sure taught me more! Expect to have your horizons broadened
and your thinking challenged."
—Warren W. Wiersbe, author and conference speaker

"This is more than a sampling of edifying and rewarding evangelical literature. It will promote and encourage worthwhile reading habits and will
call evangelicals to higher ground."
—Carl F. H. Henry, founding editor of *Christianity Today*,
evangelical theologian, and author

"You have chosen wisely. Delving into your pages is like meeting some of
God's greatest servants in our own time."
—Dr. Sherwood E. Wirt, founding editor, *Decision* magazine

"'Of the making of many books there is no end,' the Preacher said (Eccles.
12:12). Indeed! But which ones should we actually READ? The best answer
to this is: the most influential ones, of course! But what are they? Here we
have 100 of the most significant Christian books of the century."
—Walter Elwell, Wheaton College

"This is a fascinating way to present history—through the people and ideas
of the 20th century. The Petersens have done us a huge service."
—Marshall Shelley, vice president, editorial, *Christianity Today*

"One of my first ever pieces of published writing was a review of one of
William J. Petersen's earlier works, *Another Hand on Mine*. Now more than
thirty years and a lifetime of stellar works later comes this compendium of
insight. . . . After exposure to the summaries of these pivotal works, you too
will begin scouring your favorite sources for classics that not only changed
the twentieth century, but which also are destined to change your life."
—Jerry Jenkins, author and writer-at-large, Moody Bible Institute

100
Christian Books That Changed the Century

WILLIAM J. PETERSEN
and RANDY PETERSEN

Fleming H. Revell
A Division of Baker Book House Co
Grand Rapids, Michigan 49516

Published by Fleming H. Revell
a division of Baker Book House
P.O. Box 6287, Grand Rapids, MI 49516–6287

Printed in the United States of America

Library of Congress Cataloging-in-Publication Data

Petersen, William J.
    100 Christian books that changed the century / William J. Petersen and Randy Petersen.
      p.   cm.
    Includes index.
    ISBN 0-8007-5735-1
    1. Christian literature—History and criticism. 2. Literature, Modern—20th century. I. Title: One hundred Christian books that changed the century. II. Petersen, Randy. III. Title.

BR117.P48 2000
270.8'2—dc21
                                      00–030500

For current information about all releases from Baker Book House, visit our web site:
                    http://www.bakerbooks.com

Contents

{ 8 }

Preface

This is an exploration of the one hundred most influential Christian books of the twentieth century. Compiling any list like this requires some hubris. We have no special wisdom that gives us the right to anoint one book and reject another, but we want to present our opinion as a conversation piece, if nothing else. Others may wish to add another hundred to our list—fine. We just thought we'd take a look at how specific books have shaped Christians in the past hundred years.

A few cautions:

- These are not necessarily the *best* books, but those that have helped to shape people, other thinkers and writers, churches, movements, and society in general.

- We recognize that we have an evangelical bias to our selections, because we're evangelicals. Yet among the various branches of Christianity, the evangelicals seem to have done the most with books in this century. Still, we have listed a few from the Catholic or mainline Protestant community as well.

- In many cases, a particular author has written several influential books. We've tried to choose just one of those books, which stands for the author's whole output. Exceptions are when a single author has had different *kinds* of influences, such as C. S. Lewis with *Mere Christianity, The Chronicles of Narnia,* and *The Screwtape Letters.*

- We have also tried to find a balance throughout the century. Often people assume that recent best-sellers are the best books ever, even though they haven't stood the test of time. So we've made a point of selecting some lesser-known (but still important) books from the earlier decades. It's interesting that the 1990s have turned out to be the least-represented decade, largely because it's too soon to tell the full influence its books will have. (Perhaps it's also because modern movers and shakers have turned to other media.)

- The list starts with a book published in 1899, *In His Steps.* That's no typo. We included it because its phenomenal influence was seen throughout the twentieth century, even today in the WWJD (What Would Jesus Do?) craze.

In preparing our list, we consulted with a number of experts. They helped us identify some important books we had overlooked and convinced us to cross a few off the list—but we didn't always take their advice. So don't blame them if you don't agree with our admittedly subjective collection of books.

Still, we owe deep thanks to Larry and Lois Sibley, Mark Noll, Stephen Board, Martin Marty, James Reapsome, Marshall Shelley, and Floyd Thatcher.

We also want to thank our wife and mother, Ardythe Petersen, for her support and helpful input. Also, the book was her idea.

In His Steps

1899

CHARLES SHELDON

A new century was about to dawn. Some people had prophe-
sied that it would be a millennial century, a Christian century.
Charles Sheldon, pastor of Central Congregational Church in
Topeka, Kansas, hoped for that too.

The last half of the nineteenth century had been a time of
evangelistic fervor. But what concerned Sheldon was not conversion as much as consecration. He wanted to see a Christian
lifestyle. Were his church members living as Jesus lived? Was
society being changed? If people were being saved, why weren't
they affecting their communities?

The problems of immigration, urbanization, and industrial-
ization were causing social disorder and unrest throughout the
country. A few Christians were doing something about the problems. In Chicago, Jane Addams had started Hull House in the
slums; in Columbus, Ohio, Washington Gladden called for a
religion of relevance and for its "application to all human relations." And in Topeka, then a city of thirty-three thousand people, Charles Sheldon began writing a book on the simple theme,
What would Jesus do?

It's not great literature, but the story is built on a great idea.
The main character, Rev. Henry Maxwell, challenges his church
members to "pledge themselves, earnestly and honestly for an
entire year, not to do anything without first asking the question,
'What would Jesus do?'" The book then traces the lives of various church members throughout the year.

As he was writing, Sheldon read the book to his youth group
on Sunday evenings to test it out—one chapter per week. Because
the response was so enthusiastic, and because adults as well as
teens wanted to hear each new installment, Sheldon sent the
manuscript to three book publishers. All rejected it.

So Sheldon asked his denominational paper, the *Chicago Advocate*, to put it in print, and it did, one chapter per issue. When the installments were completed, they were combined and published as a ten-cent paperback—selling one hundred thousand copies in just a few weeks.

Suddenly other publishers were eager to put it into print, including some publishers that had previously rejected it. And because the denominational magazine was not copyrighted, sixteen U.S. publishers (and many more in Europe and Australia) soon published their own editions of *In His Steps*. Sheldon never got royalties on his smash hit but he wasn't bitter. Instead, he seemed thankful that the message of the book was reaching millions of readers. In midcentury *Publisher's Weekly* reported that its sales topped those of every book except the Bible.

In 1900, after *In His Steps* was published, the publisher of the local newspaper asked Sheldon to edit the paper—as Jesus might do—for one week. Sheldon screened both the editorial and advertising copy closely and ruled out liquor and tobacco ads. Though the newspaper's circulation increased, Sheldon's policies weren't continued.

Sheldon remained pastor of the Topeka church until 1919, when at the age of sixty-two he retired from the ministry and became editor of the *Christian Herald* magazine for six years. He wrote numerous books, most of them exhibiting his concern for the social implications of the gospel.

Amazingly *In His Steps* was a best-seller not only in the first decade of the twentieth century but also in the last. The 1990s saw teenagers rallying around the book, wearing "WWJD" (Sheldon's theme, What would Jesus do?) on bracelets, T-shirts, even tattoos. Few books of Christian fiction have had such staying power or have impacted as many lives.

Its simple message strikes home in any era. As Reverend Maxwell preaches at the book's conclusion: "If our definition of being a Christian is simply to enjoy the privileges of worship, be generous at no expense to ourselves, have a good, easy time surrounded by pleasant friends and by comfortable things, live respectably, and at the same time avoid the world's great stress of sin and trouble—if this is our definition of Christianity, surely we are a long way from following the steps of Him who trod the way with tears of anguish for a lost humanity."

The Evangelization of the World in This Generation

1900

JOHN R. MOTT

In 1885 participants at the annual Northfield (Massachusetts) Conference, hosted by famous evangelist D. L. Moody, were challenged to evangelize the world. Moody jumped to his feet and asked the audience, "How many of you believe this can be done?" When he got an enthusiastic response, he called for a small group to work out the details of how to do it. In that group was a young man from Iowa named John R. Mott.

Three years later Mott and three others launched the Student Volunteer Movement, taking as its motto, "Evangelization of the world in this generation." Still in his twenties, Mott began to speak at American colleges, perhaps the first to concentrate on campus evangelism. Soon Moody's organization named Mott as the great preacher's heir apparent, though their styles of evangelism were quite different. As one of Mott's associates put it, "Mott addressed himself to the reason, the conscience and the will—not to the emotions. He could not touch the heart of the man in the street, as Moody could. But Mott's method appealed to critical students." Mott, a Cornell grad, was starting Bible study groups in Ivy League schools. He had a way of answering the questions of agnostics, leading them to Christ.

By 1895, when Mott was barely thirty, he was circling the world; mobilizing Christian students in Europe, Asia, Australia; launching the World Student Christian Federation; and challenging students to reach the world for Christ in their generation.

But student evangelism was only part of Mott's larger passion: world evangelism. In the fall of 1900, he published a 210-page book that became a manual of the missionary movement, containing what one reviewer said was "an array of missionary information such as can be found in no other book of its size." Before long, it was translated into half a dozen languages. Trying to explain its success, some said it was nineteenth-century optimism mixed with an Old Testament prophetic thrust and Mott's driving sense of crisis, duty, and sensitivity to the world's needs.

In the book Mott reviewed the history of world evangelization, emphasized its biblical basis, and cited famous missionaries who endorsed the idea. He then listed facts, figures, and forecasts from leading authorities. "Practically the whole world is open," he said. The church has unprecedented resources and it is "entirely possible to fill the earth with the knowledge of Christ before the present generation passes away." The methods Mott proposed were cutting edge, as he called for highly qualified volunteers, teamwork with the indigenous church, cooperation among agencies, greater support from home churches, and more awareness of the missionary cause in theological seminaries.

{ 16 }

It's hard to distinguish between the effect of Mott's personal dynamism and the influence of the book, but the book was a battle cry that resounded through Protestant churches—"Evangelization of the world in this generation." About a year after the book came out, there were 1,173 missionary volunteers sailing overseas under 46 societies to 53 countries. Two years later the total had swelled to 1,953 volunteers for overseas missions. By World War I, the total was 5,000. By World War II, 25,000 had made their way overseas, motivated by Mott's Student Volunteer Movement and the battle cry of this book.

For half a century John Mott stood at the forefront of Christian efforts in missions and student evangelism. He's been dubbed "Protestantism's leading statesman," and the "father of the modern ecumenical movement" (because of his role as chairman of the 1910 Edinburgh Assembly, which later turned into the International Missionary Conference, out of which eventually sprang the World Council of Churches). A Japanese leader called him "the father of the young people of the world." President Woodrow Wilson wanted to name him ambassador to China, but he turned it down. In 1946, at the age of eighty-one, he was awarded the Nobel Peace Prize.

But despite all the acclaim, Mott's main thesis was always a simple one: "The primary work of the Church is to make Jesus Christ known and obeyed and loved throughout the world."

Quiet Talks on Power

1901

S. D. GORDON

At the dawn of the century, most people were fascinated by *power*. There was no doubt that the coming years would be dominated by how power could be harnessed. In recent decades, revolutions had occurred in transportation (with the steam engine and combustion engine), in communications (with the telegraph, telephone, wireless, and transatlantic cable), and even in domestic life (with electric lights, sewing machines, and phonographs). The key to it all was power.

In the world at large, America had become a world power, defeating Spain in Cuba and in the Philippines. And with its new president, Teddy Roosevelt, who claimed to speak softly but carry a big stick, the country's status as a world power was destined to continue.

Maybe in spiritual matters too the country looked for someone who could speak softly but show the way to power. Some preachers used Victorian English to explain how to live the Christian life. Some evangelists ranted and raved about getting saved and walking down the sawdust trail. But many Christians wanted some straightforward how-to-do-it answers about what their faith was all about.

Quiet Talks on Power was the first in a twenty-one-volume *Quiet Talks* series by S. D. Gordon, published over the next thirty years. The best-seller of the series was *Quiet Talks on Prayer*, published in 1904; it has sold well over a half million copies and is still in print. Others in the series include *Quiet Talks on Service, Quiet Talks on the Lord's Return, Quiet Talks on Witnessing,* and *Quiet Talks on Jesus.* Combined sales of the series top the three million mark.

Yet the books' significance rests not in their spectacular sales but in Gordon's down-to-earth way of communicating with ordinary people. One of the earliest reviews spoke of Gordon's style as "full of power" and "charged with an electric current." Another said that Gordon had made "familiar truths lively and intensely practical." These were not Christian books for the theologically trained but for the average Joe. Gordon learned his speaking and writing style through his experience with the YMCA and he wanted to reach working men. That made Gordon's writing unusual for his time.

Samuel Dickey Gordon—always known as simply S. D.—was born in Philadelphia in 1859 and began working with the YMCA there when he was twenty-five. In 1896 he quit his job and began a four-year lecture tour around the world. When he returned, he began writing his first book, *Quiet Talks on Power.* For the next thirty years, he was much in demand as a devotional speaker and writer.

In that first book, Gordon talks about the necessity of a personal relationship with Christ and making sure that power channels are not clogged. A key chapter is "Making and Breaking Connections," in which he defines five main words used in the New Testament regarding the Holy Spirit's relation to the Christian. *Baptism* is the historical word, describing an act done once for all on Pentecost. *Filled* is the experience word; *anointed* is the purpose word; and *sealed* is the ownership or property word. And *earnest* (or *guarantee*) is the prophetic word, pointing forward to the day when Christ returns.

"Power," says Gordon, "depends on good connections. The train with the locomotive, machinery with the engine; the electrical mechanism with the powerhouse. And in the Christian life the follower of Jesus with the Spirit of Jesus."

He concludes by writing, "Fresh supplies of power are dependent upon two things. The first is this—keeping the life free of hindrances. . . . The second thing is the cultivation of personal friendship with God."

The book is filled with warm stories as well as with biblical examples. The final page tells of an eighteenth-century German theologian who would return to his room late at night and read his Bible for an hour. Then after a few minutes of silence, he would say simply, "Well, Lord, Jesus, we're on the same old terms. Good night." He was keeping the power communication channels open.

Up from Slavery

1901

BOOKER T. WASHINGTON

Booker Taliaferro Washington was born in 1856, a slave on a Virginia plantation. He was just a boy when the Emancipation Proclamation set him free. But freedom was one thing, education was another. And the entire South, including its education system, was in ruins after the Civil War. How could former slaves get ahead in the world without an education?

Fortunately some Christians saw that need and did what they could to help. The American Missionary Association (primarily Congregationalist) started industrial and agricultural schools and soon it had launched more than twenty schools, including Fisk in Tennessee and Hampton in Virginia. Then the Methodist-backed Freedmen's Aid Society and the American Baptist Home Mission Board began investing in African American education.

Blacks responded eagerly. Booker T. Washington would comment later, "It was a whole race trying to go to school. . . . Few were too young, and none too old, to make the attempt to learn. . . . The great ambition of the older people was to try to read the Bible before they died."

Washington attended the Hampton Institute and Industrial School and later Virginia and Wayland Seminary. He became a teacher and at the age of twenty-five he began Tuskegee Institute in Alabama. Under his presidency, Tuskegee became a leading center of black education. His motto: "The individual who can do something that the world wants done will, in the end, make his way regardless of his race."

The success of this bright young man as an educator earned him national attention. In 1896 he became the first African American to receive an honorary master of arts degree from Harvard. By 1900 he was known as America's most influential black leader.

In 1901 Booker T. Washington published his autobiography, *Up from Slavery*, now an American classic. (In 1999 *USA Today* listed it second among its Books of the Century.) Translated into more than fifteen languages, it communicates a positive message of overcoming adversity through hard work and clean living. "While the Negro should not be deprived by unfair means of the franchise, political agitation alone would not save him, and that back of the ballot he must have property, industry, skill, economy, intelligence and character."

Though he was roundly condemned by his fellow blacks for not taking a stronger position on civil rights and social equality, Washington felt that good race relations were more desirable than civil rights. And this book, one of the first by an African American to be popular among whites, was an eye-opener. Whites and blacks, from North and South, got a clear picture of what it meant to grow up black in the South.

In fifteen chapters *Up From Slavery* tells Washington's life story. As a child slave on a Virginia plantation, he did not know his father, never slept on a bed, and never ate a family meal with knives and forks. But he remembered waking up early one morning and hearing his mother praying that Lincoln and his armies might be successful and that one day she and her children might be free.

As a young man working in a salt mine, he heard of Hampton Institute. While a student there he learned "how to use and love the Bible." As a result of that training, he says, "I always make it a rule to read a chapter or a portion of the chapter in the morning, before beginning the work of the day."

Much of the book tells of his struggles in establishing Tuskegee Institute, which was opened in an "old dilapidated shanty." The roof leaked so much when it rained that a student had to hold an umbrella over Washington's head as he taught. But despite the difficulties, Washington never allowed himself to become bitter. "Long ago . . . I resolved that I would permit no man, no matter what his color might be, to narrow and degrade my soul by making me hate him."

It was this Christ-like attitude that helped Washington change the world. Later leaders would pick up the political struggle for equality, but this hero focused on nourishing the minds and the souls of his people—and all people.

The Crises of the Christ

1903

G. CAMPBELL MORGAN

When it came time to prepare Sunday's sermon, the average twentieth-century pastor had G. Campbell Morgan by his side more than any other author. Morgan, often called "the prince of expositors," wrote more than sixty books of scriptural com- mentary, covering the whole Bible in the process, but concentrating on the four Gospels. His classic work is *The Crises of the Christ,* one of his earliest, even though it is not really typical of his expository works.

The surprising thing is that Morgan himself had no seminary training. In fact he was rejected as a preaching candidate by both the Salvation Army and the Methodists. He floundered a while in his faith after reading Huxley and Darwin, but then he locked all his books in a cupboard, got a new Bible, and began to read it. "If it be the Word of God," he said, "and if I come to it with an unprejudiced and open mind, it will bring assurance to my soul of itself." What happened? In Morgan's words, "The Bible found me!" From that day on, he became a man of the Book.

At the age of twenty-seven, he was ordained as pastor of a small Congregational church in Staffordshire, England; two years later went to another church; and then in two more years moved on again. After serving four churches in eleven years, he came to America in 1901 to work for two years with Moody's Northfield extension ministries. Moody called him "one of the most remarkable men who ever came to Northfield." When that work was ending and he was planning to go back to his native England, he wrote his masterwork: *The Crises of the Christ.*

While most of Morgan's later books are more expositional, this one is doctrinal. As he says in his preface, his focus is not on Christ's words or works, but rather on the accomplishment of the divine work, God's eternal plan.

The subtitle sums it up: *The Seven Greatest Events of His Life.* After an introduction in which Morgan talks about man's fall into sin, he discusses in succeeding chapters Christ's birth, baptism, temptation, transfiguration, crucifixion, resurrection, and ascension. Then he concludes by showing how all of this culminates in man's redemption.

What gave the book such popularity and such lasting appeal? Morgan always wrote with clarity as well as insight. Laypeople as well as ministers actually enjoyed reading Bible exposition by Morgan. Because he avoided doctrinal controversies, his books received wide acceptance. He felt his ministry was to all the churches, not just to one.

After returning to England, Morgan took the pastorate at Westminster Chapel in London, where he stayed thirteen years—writing expository books the whole time. The church had been struggling, but under his expository preaching huge crowds began attending. In 1918 he returned to the United States, took short-term pastorates, faculty positions, and itinerant speaking engagements. Sometimes when he spoke, crowds were so large that police control was necessary. In 1933 he returned again to England, accepting the pastorate of Westminster Chapel a second time. Ten years later he retired, at the age of eighty, but not before bringing in D. Martyn Lloyd-Jones as his associate and successor. Morgan died at age eighty-two.

The Crises of the Christ stands near the beginning of an impressive body of work by this "prince of expositors." With clear communication of his insights into Scripture, G. Campbell Morgan equipped and inspired a long line of preachers, stretching throughout the twentieth century. When you're puzzling over a preaching text on Saturday night, you can always count on Morgan to give you something to say.

Hurlbut's Story of the Bible

1904

JESSE LYMAN HURLBUT

"Tell me a story, Mommy."

Hearing this, millions of Christian parents through the years have looked for books of Bible stories to share with their children. In the nineteenth century the American Sunday-School Union had published some small books of Bible stories that proved very popular, but as the twentieth century opened there was a need for a new book of Bible stories.

Jesse Lyman Hurlbut decided to meet that need. With children of his own ranging in age from six to sixteen when he wrote the book, he certainly knew a few things about kids. And he knew the Bible pretty well too. One of the founders of the Epworth League of the Methodist Church, he also served as director of the Biblical Institute of Newark, New Jersey. Throughout his life, he wrote about thirty books in all.

With about five million copies in print, Hurlbut's *Story of the Bible* "for young and old" has set the standard for others to match. Many other excellent storybooks have been published during the century, but Hurlbut's has always maintained a singular status. In the first half of the century, its sales made it the twelfth best-selling book in the United States (of all books, not just Christian books). In 1962 *Time* magazine called it "one of the best-selling religion books of all time." The John C. Winston Company published the book originally, but Zondervan Publishing House obtained rights in 1962 and has produced thirty-one printings.

Dedicated to "the Young People of America," Hurlbut tells 168 Bible stories in chronological order, so that both parents and children have a good understanding of the complete sweep of the Scriptures.

In his preface, Hurlbut explains clearly "what we aim to do." His stated goals make it clear that he loves the Scriptures, but he also has a driving passion to communicate these stories to kids in a way they'll understand. While the principles aren't revolutionary today, they help explain why the book proved so successful. The purpose of his *Story of the Bible,* Hurlbut wrote, is: (1) to tell the stories in order so that the reader has a complete Bible history; (2) to make each story complete in itself with a separate title; (3) to write in plain, but not childish language, so that a ten year old can understand it, with words like *altar, tabernacle, synagogue,* and *centurion* explained, and to exclude technical terms; (4) to remain faithful to the biblical text, to avoid imaginary scenes, and to use biblical language as much as possible, so that readers are drawn to the Bible, not away from it; (5) to avoid doctrinal issues, so that all denominations would feel at home with it; (6) to write with short paragraphs; (7) to choose illustrations with care.

We find a sample of Hurlbut's child-friendly writing in the creation story: "This great round world, on which we live, is very old, so old that no one knows when it was made. But long before there was any earth, or sun, or stars, God was living, for God never began to be. He always was."

Newer Bible story books have done more with colorful graphics, of course, but Hurlbut's basic wording has proven amazingly durable. Each new generation seems to come up with a favorite in this category: Egemeier's Bible stories in the 1930s, the brilliant Arch Concordia series in the 1960s, and others in the 1990s, but Hurlbut's remains a classic. As we enter the twenty-first century, this old book still has a following.

Power through Prayer

1907

E. M. BOUNDS

In the early years of the twentieth century President Teddy Roosevelt exuded power, inspiring Americans to believe that, whatever their circumstances, they could rise above them.

Rise above them? Of course. In the first decade of the century, skyscrapers were being built, the Wright brothers had their first successful airplane flight, and wireless telegrams were flying through the air. Was there anything we couldn't do if we really tried?

The Christian church was captured by the same philosophy. John R. Mott talked about reaching the world in this generation. Evangelist Billy Sunday talked about winning entire cities for Christ. A newly created Federal Council of Churches sought to bring about the redemption of the world by getting social justice into all areas of life. *We can do it,* they said.

In the small town of Washington, Georgia, lived a retired Methodist minister who began each day with three hours of prayer. If you forget prayer, he said, you won't accomplish anything.

This man knew about accomplishments. Edwin McKendree Bounds had attended a one-room school in Shelbyville, Missouri, but became a lawyer before he turned nineteen. After practicing law for five years, he felt the call to preach. Soon he was pastoring a Southern Methodist Church, but during the Civil War, he was arrested by Union troops, charged as a Confederate sympathizer, and jailed for about eighteen months. After the war he served churches in Tennessee, Alabama, and back in Missouri, but then he turned to the written word—as associate editor of the *Christian Advocate,* the nationwide weekly magazine for Methodists.

When he was nearly sixty years old, he and his family moved to Washington, Georgia, where he spent his time engaged in prayer and writing and in an itinerant revival ministry. Each morning he awoke at 4 A.M. to be alone with God for a few hours.

His close friend Homer W. Hodge helped him get his writings published. All told, eleven books by Bounds reached print, seven of these on the subject of prayer. Said Hodge, "There is no man that has lived since the days of the Apostles that has surpassed him in the depths of his marvelous research into the life of prayer."

Power through Prayer (originally called *Preacher and Prayer*) was the only one of his seven prayer books to be published before his death but it gained a worldwide audience (causing Hodge to dust off other Bounds books on prayer). Bounds was writing for ministers, but the book is applicable to all. In twenty short chapters, the old lawyer makes the case for prayer. It's a pep talk more than a how-to and it's filled with memorable aphorisms.

"The Holy Ghost does not flow through methods, but through men," Bounds writes in chapter 1. "He does not come on machinery, but on men. He does not anoint plans, but men— men of prayer." The chapter concludes with what might well be Bounds's theme sentence: "Every preacher who does not make prayer a mighty factor in his own life and ministry is weak as a factor in God's work and is powerless to project God's cause in the world."

In the final chapters he urges ministers to inspire their congregations to pray for them. "Where are the Christly leaders who can teach the modern saints how to pray and put them at it? . . . We are not a generation of praying saints. Nonpraying saints are a beggarly gang who have neither the ardor nor the beauty nor the power of saints."

On page after page of this concise book, Bounds is both eminently quotable and pointedly challenging. British evangelist Leonard Ravenhill wrote: "Bounds's writings on prayer have never been equaled." *Power through Prayer* has deeply influenced the lives of thousands of pastors as well as laypeople. Translated into many languages, it remains in print after nearly a century and continues to sell briskly today.

The Scofield Reference Bible

1909

C. I. SCOFIELD

Walk through the Bible section of a bookstore these days (or scroll through a bookstore's web site) and you'll find study Bibles of all shapes and sizes, for all ages, interests, and theological leanings. Today Bibles with notes are commonplace, and dozens of Bibles cater to different audiences. But prior to the Scofield Bible, an annotated Bible was a rarity.

In fact the translators of the 1611 King James Version of the Bible had been told, "No marginal notes are to be affixed," except notes relating to Hebrew and Greek. That attitude held for three centuries. And until about 1970, the Scofield Reference Bible was unique, virtually the only study Bible available. Many readers accepted Scofield's notes as gospel truth. After all, it was in the Bible—the Scofield Bible. (In the 1960s, some were singing, tongue-in-cheek, "My hope is built on nothing less than Scofield notes and Scripture Press.)

A lawyer who had served in the Kansas legislature, C. I. Scofield left his law practice to enter the ministry when he was thirty-nine, shortly after his conversion. He became pastor of a small church in Dallas, Texas, which grew rapidly under his Bible-teaching ministry. Evangelist D. L. Moody took note of him and Scofield became Moody's pastor for seven years in Massachusetts. Then he went back to his previous church in Dallas. When he was nearing his sixtieth birthday, Scofield began working on a reference Bible. His purpose: to help people study Scriptures systematically. The church eventually gave Scofield a leave of absence and he finished his reference Bible in time for it to be published in 1909.

In preparation he consulted with an eight-member panel of consulting editors, most of whom, but not all, shared his theological leanings. Scofield's theology was strongly dispensationalist. Dispensationalism is based on the idea that God has worked progressively in seven different dispensations, each characterized by a different divine promise, a different test, and mankind's failure to meet God's standards. Scofield also held to a pre-Adamic race and a gap between Genesis 1:1 and 1:2. Regarding the second coming of Christ, Scofield taught that there would be a rapture of the church before a seven-year tribulation, which would be followed by a thousand-year millennium.

Although many Bible scholars quarreled with nuances of its theology, the Scofield Bible got Christians studying the Word of God as never before and gave them handles on which to hang their beliefs. And even those who don't share his obvious dispensationalist views can find benefit in Scofield's thorough chain-references, definitions, and summaries.

In 1917 some of the rough edges of the Scofield Bible were removed in a "new and improved edition," which remained the standard Scofield version until 1967, when a Revised Scofield Bible was published. In 1976 the Ryrie Study Bible was published, which was a further adaptation of Scofield's original.

One critic of the Scofield Bible said: "It may fairly be called one of the most influential books—perhaps it is the most influential single book—thrust into the religious life of America during the twentieth century."

He may well have been right. Interestingly enough, when the revised edition of the Scofield Bible was published in 1967, its influence began to wane, but until then it was the Bible of choice for most evangelicals. It had shaped the thinking of many Christians for two generations.

Missionary Methods:
St. Paul's or Ours

1912

ROLAND ALLEN

In the first half of the century, the methods of foreign missions were not questioned or analyzed. In many parts of the world, missionaries were still pioneers, sometimes venturing into unexplored lands or preaching the gospel to people steeped in other religions.

When Roland Allen published this questioning book, it had been less than forty years since David Livingstone had been traipsing around the heart of Africa, and exactly a century since the first American missionaries, Adoniram and Ann Judson, had gone to Rangoon, Burma. At that time in history, missionary-minded Christians were just glad that someone was doing *something;* they weren't analyzing to see if it was being done right.

But that was precisely what Roland Allen did. "Are we actually planting new churches or merely perpetuating a mission?" he asked. "And at what stage in church building does a missionary become dispensable?"

Roland Allen knew what he was talking about, having served as an Anglican missionary in northern China from 1895 to 1903, working under the Society for the Propagation of the Gospel. He returned to take a British parish church and devote himself to writing on missionary principles, as well as editing a magazine on missions. From that observation post, he began asking tough questions about mission work. And he pulled no punches.

Missionary Methods: St. Paul's or Ours has five parts. The first examines how the apostle Paul went into the major cities of his day, the conditions of ministry in that day, and how they compared to modern times. The second part looks at how Paul presented the gospel and asks questions about Paul's financial policy of self-support for himself and the new churches—comparing once again to twentieth-century practices. The third part discusses how Paul trained converts and the rapid way in which he appointed leaders, contrasting that with the slow and cautious way it was being done in Allen's day. Fourth, the book considers authority and discipline in the churches and asks whether missionaries have imported western systems rather than biblical ones. And finally, Allen draws some conclusions, charging that "we can more easily believe in His work in us and through us than we can believe in His work in and through our converts." Even where missionary efforts have been carried on for several generations, he notes, Christianity is still viewed as an import, an exotic, foreign commodity. "We have allowed racial and religious pride to direct our attitudes," he says. "We have lacked faith in the work of the Spirit."

As you might guess, Allen's criticisms were unappreciated at first. John R. Mott at the time was leading the crusade to "evangelize the world in this generation." To pay too much attention to proper methods would just slow down the process. Still, there were enough enthusiastic readers to help the book survive through several printings and editions.

Allen was clearly ahead of his time. The changes he called for were slow in coming. In fact, before he died in 1947, Allen said that he expected that it would take until 1960 before people would really take him seriously. That's about what happened.

Actually a number of mission leaders were taking Allen seriously all along, but bureaucracies take a long time to implement change, and old methods die hard—especially when we feel God is working through them. But the 1960s and 1970s began to see major changes in mission work. In particular, missionaries have shifted their efforts toward supporting the national church in the areas they're serving. They are less apt to impose Western methods of worship, instruction, or evangelism and more apt to accept local methods. Mission agencies have taken a hard look at their traditional methods, asking themselves how to make missions more biblical.

This quiet revolution in missionary work is largely due to Roland Allen and his courageous book. In his introduction to the latest edition, Lesslie Newbigin of the Church of South India wrote, "Quietly but insistently, [this book] has continued to challenge the accepted assumptions of churches and missions, and slowly but steadily the number of those who found themselves compelled to listen has increased."

War on the Saints

1912

JESSIE PENN-LEWIS

If you thought spiritual warfare was something that someone thought up in the 1980s, you're dead wrong. The classic in the field is a book written early in the century by a woman from Wales named Jessie Penn-Lewis. *War on the Saints* is the definitive book on biblical demonology and satanic warfare.

Penn-Lewis was known for other writings as well. When the ninety essays that composed *The Fundamentals* were written a few years later to address the modernist threat in America, only one was written by a woman—Jessie Penn-Lewis.

She was surprising in other ways too. She had no theological education and she took a strong stand for a woman's place in church ministries, even though it was not a popular position among fundamentalists of her day.

Born in England in 1861, she married an accountant at the age of nineteen and was converted to Christianity when she was twenty-one. Although she suffered from a lung ailment, she accepted a position with the YWCA. Her success as an organizer of Bible classes took her throughout England.

The first material she had published was a booklet called *The Pathway to Life in God,* which sold thirty-two thousand copies in five years. Soon she was asked to speak in Scandinavia, Russia, Switzerland, and South Africa. In Russia she felt demonic opposition to her message and afterwards wrote *Conflict in the Heavenlies.*

In 1903 she helped launch a Keswick Convention in Llandrindod Wells, Wales. This triggered an amazing revival. Crowds swarmed to the area. After a two-hour sermon, the meetings would last until 2:30 in the morning with praying and singing. "Shopkeepers are closing early in order to get a place in the chapel," the Cardiff newspaper reported, "and tin and steel workers throng the place in working clothes." As the revival spread into other communities, Jessie Penn-Lewis shared in the leadership of the movement. But in 1905 she felt that Satan seemed to be trying to counterfeit true revival. She wanted to answer the threat in the best way she knew how—by writing the truth. In consultation with revival leader Evan Roberts, she incorporated material from her previous work, *Conflict in the Heavenlies,* and wrote her classic *War on the Saints.*

Only three thousand copies were printed in the first edition and it sold out quickly. So Jessie added more material to the second edition, and the sales of it were remarkable. The book has continued to sell throughout the century. It includes (1) a biblical survey of satanic deception, (2) an understanding of how evil spirits work today, (3) an explanation of satanic deception and possession, (4) the path to freedom, (5) how to obtain victory in the conflict, (6) war on the powers of darkness, (7) and revival on the horizon.

Although her book on how Satan works wasn't the first such book published in the century (missionary J. L. Nevius's work on demon possession in China preceded hers), she became known as the authority in the field, and when the editors of *The Fundamentals* wanted someone to write on Satan and his kingdom, they turned to Jessie Penn-Lewis.

Though not well-known today, Jessie Penn-Lewis has influenced the modern church in several ways. First, she was one of the first women to be recognized as an authority on a matter of Christian doctrine. There were other prominent female writers, but Penn-Lewis was hailed as an expert. Second, she wielded great influence in the Welsh Revival, which was a key event in the burgeoning Pentecostal movement. And finally, *War on the Saints* remains a classic on spiritual warfare, a subject that keeps resurfacing in modern times.

International Standard Bible Encyclopedia

1915

JAMES ORR, GENERAL EDITOR

It is still called ISBE (pronounced "Izzbe") and any book that is known by its initials eighty years after its publication has to rate { 33 } as one of the most influential of the century.

First published in five volumes (3,500 pages), this encyclopedia continues to enjoy steady sales, having influenced evangelical pastors and lay leaders throughout the past century. In the 1980s, under the editorship of Geoffrey Bromiley, a major revision was issued, thus ensuring that it would continue to serve students of Scripture well into the twenty-first century.

Scotsman James Orr took the responsibility as general editor of the first edition because he believed there was a need for a reference work "adapted more directly to the needs of the average pastor and Bible student." By going into things in more depth than a Bible dictionary would and by discussing a broader range of issues, Orr was able to provide evangelical pastors and theologians with an orthodox line of defense when they felt that liberal theology was winning the war.

Orr was an amazing scholar who made his impact on the twentieth century through a number of books. Born in Glasgow, Scotland, in 1844, Orr first achieved status as a theologian and philosopher with his book, *The Christian View of God and the World, as Centring in the Incarnation,* published in 1893. This volume, sometimes called his classic work, presents a case for a Christian worldview that interprets life more satisfactorily than any other philosophy or religion. In other words, it makes sense. Besides that, he argued that the incarnation was nonnegotiable. Without it, Christianity wouldn't be Christianity anymore.

Later Orr wrote books on inspiration and on evolution, not espousing a hard view on inerrancy nor against evolution.

Although he refused to take a position on "a hard-and-fast inerrancy in minute matters of historical, geographical, chronological and scientific detail," he felt that the degree of accuracy is so high that this accuracy is in itself an argument for the supernatural origin of Scripture. But in his works on the virgin birth and the resurrection, he strongly attested to the centrality of these Christian doctrines. To abandon belief in the virgin birth is tantamount to abandoning belief in the doctrine of Christ's deity, Orr believed. He also contributed four articles to *The Fundamentals,* as the battle between conservatives and liberals was coming to a head.

Far from being an ivory-tower theologian, James Orr wrote for city newspapers as well as for theological journals, and while lecturing at prestigious seminaries, he went outside to speak on open-air platforms about the basics of the Christian faith.

But his enduring legacy may be in ISBE, which is not only a steadfast defense of orthodoxy, but also provides pastors and laypeople with the knowledge they need to stand for an evangelical faith. As theologian Glen Scorgie puts it, the *International Standard Bible Encyclopedia* "has stamped his influence on several generations of conservative Protestant pastors and leaders in North America."

The Fundamentals

1919

A. C. DIXON, LOUIS MEYER,
and R. A. TORREY, GENERAL EDITORS

No matter what edition you want to consider, this work made a significant mark on the century both spiritually and socially. It appeared first as ninety articles, then in twelve small books, and then again in four volumes. The material is uneven in style and covers a hodgepodge of subject matter but its totality provided a foundation for fundamentalists to stand on when they seemed to be losing the war with liberalism.

{ 35 }

The project began in 1909 when two wealthy Christian laymen in Los Angeles "set aside money to issue twelve volumes that would set forth the fundamentals of the faith." Originally the idea was to distribute copies of the booklets free of charge "to every pastor, evangelist, missionary, theological student, Sunday school superintendent, and YMCA and YWCA secretary in the English-speaking world, so far as the addresses of these could be obtained." More than three million copies were eventually circulated. Eventually the funds ran out, and so the materials were published and sold in book form.

A. C. Dixon took the job as the first executive secretary and general editor of the project, but soon he received a call to pastor Spurgeon's Metropolitan Tabernacle in London and had to resign the post. His successor was Louis Meyer, who died after two years in office. Then the job was given to R. A. Torrey, dean of the Bible Institute of Los Angeles, who saw the project through to completion.

The problem was this: The whole world, it seemed, was turning away from the basics of Christian doctrine—and even the churches were being swayed in this direction. Of course Charles Darwin had challenged the traditional concept of creation but he was just one of numerous scholars who were teaching new ideas that contradicted the Bible. Only ignorant people still believed those old myths—that was the attitude sweeping the United States at the time. Especially frustrating was the fact that even churches were buying into this mind-set. Denominational leaders and seminary professors were scuttling their belief in the authority of the Scriptures and teaching others to do the same.

Thus the job of Dixon, Meyer, and ultimately Torrey was to get the best minds in fundamentalism to present the conservative Christian position on the basics of the faith. These articles would set the standard for a biblical belief system and they would also demonstrate that you don't have to be uneducated and unsophisticated to believe the Bible. About seventy different topflight experts were asked to write ninety papers.

The first section dealt with higher criticism and the Bible, with authors like theologian James Orr, archaeologist G. Frederick Wright, and lawyer Robert Anderson. The next section examined the critical views of specific books of Scripture—Genesis, Daniel, the Gospel of John, and Isaiah, for instance. Next came a look at the inspiration of Scripture, and this was followed by papers dealing with various key doctrines—the incarnation, deity, and virgin birth of Christ; his bodily resurrection; and the Holy Spirit. Then came a lengthy series of papers on various aspects of salvation—atonement, propitiation, regeneration, conversion, and justification. Next the book moved into areas of church ministry—Sunday school, foreign missions, prayer, evangelism, and the nature of the true church. There was a section on modern thought, which included papers on Darwinism, evolution, and socialism, and another section on cults like Mormonism, Christian Science, and Spiritualism. In the last section there were two articles dealing with the second coming of Christ, as well as some personal testimonies of individuals.

On the whole, the papers emphasized the defense of the faith, the verbal inspiration of the Scriptures, the substitutionary theory of atonement, and the necessity of conversion. But the variety is surprising. In the midst of the theological wrangling, for instance, one paper dealt with the prayer life of the noted orphanage manager George Müller of Bristol, England. (It's also surprising that only two papers out of ninety dealt with eschatology and that only three dealt with evolution, despite the fact that these later became key subjects of interest and debate within fundamentalism.)

The Fundamentals probably didn't entice many liberals back into the conservative camp, but the writers did mark out the borders of that camp. In so doing, they defined a movement that didn't have much of an identity before this. Why are fundamentalists called fundamentalists? Because of the publication of *The Fundamentals*. Once the issues were set forth, a huge group of Bible-believing Christians knew what they stood for. And for that reason alone, *The Fundamentals* changed the century.

Christianity and Liberalism

1923

J. GRESHAM MACHEN

You'd have to admit that J. Gresham Machen was an unlikely standard-bearer for fundamentalism. In the first place, he didn't like the word; to him, it sounded too much like "some strange new sect." He also disagreed with most fundamentalists on their view of the second coming. Besides all of that, the most publicized event of the decade was the Scopes evolution trial in Tennessee, and Machen wasn't sure whether God might have used evolution in the whole creation scenario. But he did agree that the Bible was the Word of God and he did agree that the historic Christian doctrines were as true as ever.

In spite of all of Machen's differences with the fundamentalist movement, after his *Christianity and Liberalism* was published, the scholarly Machen was in demand as fundamentalism's spokesman. Famous journalists H. L. Mencken and Walter Lippman acknowledged his arguments. Major newspapers and magazines asked him for his opinions in behalf of fundamentalism. Fundamentalist conventions invited him to their platforms. Later, historian Sydney Ahlstrom called his book the "chief theological ornament of American fundamentalism."

Machen, born in 1881 and the son of a prominent Baltimore lawyer, was raised a Presbyterian, got a degree from Princeton Theological Seminary in 1905, and began teaching there a year later.

In 1923, as the fundamentalism-liberalism controversy was nearing its zenith, Machen was deeply troubled. He expressed his views in a paper for the *Princeton Theological Review,* and the paper received such a response that Machen was asked to expand it into a book. He did. The battle being waged, he said, was hampered by "low visibility." Liberals were confusing the issues. Writing in language that laypeople as well as ministers could understand, he charged that modern liberalism was both un-Christian and unscientific.

Then Machen made his case about why doctrine is important, how liberalism distorts the doctrines of God and humanity, how liberalism cheats in its study of Scripture, and how liberalism does not understand the biblical views of Christ, salvation, or the church. Christianity, he said, "must be abandoned altogether unless at a definite point in history Jesus died as a propitiation for the sins of men."

And while he disagreed with Methodists and with Roman Catholics on doctrinal matters, he said, he had much more in common with them than he had with some of his fellow Presbyterians who did not accept the authority of Scripture.

The book caused an earthquake of reaction, not only because of what Machen said, but also because of who Machen was. Liberals could dismiss other attacks from fundamentalists, but Machen was a Princeton Seminary professor, a loyal Presbyterian. On the other side, fundamentalists were heartened to find a new and important ally with high academic credentials within a major mainline denomination.

Within the Presbyterian church, Machen soon became a threat. Following the book's publication, he called for the removal of liberals from the denomination. When the denomination didn't respond, Machen broke away, founding Westminster Theological Seminary in 1929. After being expelled from the denomination in 1936, he helped to found the Presbyterian Church of America in 1936 (which later split into the Orthodox Presbyterian and Bible Presbyterian denominations). He died the following year at the age of fifty-six.

Machen's book remains an important document in the ongoing modernist-fundamentalist controversy. His passion for the purity of doctrine led him to pioneer something we might call "subdenominationalism," which has by now begun to make denominations irrelevant. Nowadays many church people would agree with Machen. They feel more of a bond with people of other denominations who share their conservative (or liberal) views on the basics of Christianity than with people in their own denomination who don't. This has sparked the start-up of numerous subdenominations and many cross-denominational alliances.

Halley's Pocket Bible Handbook

1924

HENRY H. HALLEY

Henry H. Halley had a unique gift and a unique ministry. He could memorize Scripture, chapter after chapter of it. And as his ministry, he would go into churches, recite chapters from memory, and explain the context of the passage. You might say that he was a Bible teacher with a difference.

It all started when he had to take a trip from his home in Kalamazoo, Michigan, to California. It was a long train ride, and as he was staring out the window at the sagebrush in western Kansas, he decided to quote Scripture to himself. He was surprised how much he knew. Then he used the time to memorize other passages. One Sunday he was asked to substitute in the pulpit for a pastor who was sick and he chose to quote Scripture the entire time. His presentation was so well received that he began doing what he called "Bible recitals" in other churches.

Before reciting a passage, Halley would give his audience a background sketch of the passage. One day as he was making his presentation in a church, a woman in the front row was scribbling notes and shuffling papers, distracting him and the entire congregation. So he resolved to print up some notes for free distribution, and that's the way *Halley's Pocket Bible Handbook* got started.

Henry H. Halley printed a 16-page booklet under this title in 1924, not dreaming what the future would hold. Somehow in his church ministry he sold 10,000 copies. The next year he expanded the booklet to 32 pages and printed another 10,000 copies. Then (as he writes in the foreword to the twenty-fourth edition), it kept expanding. "Then 40 [pages]. Then 80. Then 120. Then 144. Then 160." And the print runs kept growing too. In 1941 he printed 30,000 and by 1948 it had grown to 60,000.

Eventually it became an 860-page volume with average annual sales of 200,000. Total sales are now above the five million mark, with 90 printings and 25 editions, not to mention its publication in more than a dozen foreign countries. In 1960 Zondervan Publishing House became Halley's publisher, giving the handbook access to even broader channels of distribution. A new edition using the New International Version text is now available.

From the start, Halley says, the book was designed not "as a textbook, but rather as a handy brief manual of a popular nature for the average Bible reader, who has few or no commentaries or reference works on the Bible." Though the material has been greatly expanded, the core is still a brief explanation of each chapter in the Bible. More than 80 percent deals with his chapter-by-chapter summaries. But he adds to these summaries other fascinating material—such as all the references to angels in the Bible (inserted after angels ministered to Jesus after his temptation), and a chronology of the Gospels to help the reader put the events of Christ's life into place. At the end of Revelation, Halley draws twelve parallels to the early chapters of Genesis, closing with "Man's primeval home was by a river (Gen. 2:10); Man's Eternal Home will be beside a River (Rev. 22:1)."

Though not a trained theologian, Halley consulted archaeologists and seminary professors to help him update his material with each edition. After his death, Zondervan continued the practice of providing updated material.

So the handbook continues to be a helpful resource for thousands of Bible students, containing notes on each book of the Bible, explanations of obscure passages, an outline of archaeological discoveries, an "epitome" of church history and a section that Halley called "THE MOST IMPORTANT THING IN THIS BOOK." What he deemed most important was that "each church have a congregational plan of Bible reading." This was something that he had promoted in his itinerant church ministry and he resolved to continue to promote it through his book.

For many Christians, Halley's handbook is the only Bible reference book they have, and after nearly eighty years its popularity shows no signs of abating.

Orthodoxy

1925

G. K. CHESTERTON

At the portal of the modern world stood a young defender of the faith, Gilbert Keith Chesterton. As the twentieth century began, it was becoming fashionable to question the traditional Christian faith that had held the Western world in its grip. Marx and Darwin had sown their seeds and now skepticism was growing. In England literary lions like George Bernard Shaw and H. G. Wells advanced the notion that Christianity belonged to a darker age. The new world of the twentieth century would certainly feast on more intelligent fare.

Chesterton started out as an illustrator but soon he blossomed as a writer. G. K. became known as a novelist, but also as a literary critic and social commentator. *Orthodoxy* was conceived in 1903, when a man named Robert Blatchford published an attack on belief in God. Chesterton fired off a few essays in response but also began gathering thoughts for a fuller reply. It came to birth in 1908 as a series of magazine articles but was not published in book form until 1925.

The book begins with the plot of an unwritten novel: A man sails from England, hoping to explore the South Seas; but he gets turned around and ends up back in England, thinking these are South Sea Islands. "I am that man," says Chesterton, explaining the kind of faith he was looking for, the faith he found in Christianity, which was there all along.

He wanted something that captured the paradoxes of the human race. Christianity, he found, did this like no other philosophy or religion. ("Christianity alone has felt that God, to be wholly God, must have been a rebel as well as a king.")

He wanted joy, and he found it in the carpenter of Nazareth. ("Joy, which was the small publicity of the pagan, is the gigantic secret of the Christian.")

He wanted something magical and poetic, unlike the grim naturalism that was taking over the world. See how easily he makes his case for faith: "I felt in my bones; first, that this world does not explain itself. . . . The thing is magic, true or false. Second, I came to feel as if magic must have a meaning, and meaning must have someone to mean it. . . . Third, I thought this purpose beautiful in its old design. . . . Fourth, that the proper form of thanks to it is some form of humility and restraint. . . . We owed, also, an obedience to whatever made us." He takes this journey in half a page.

Chesterton's whimsical style is matched only by his biting wit. (These combine to make him one of the most quotable writers in history.) He regularly cut to the core of his opponents' arguments and exposed their inconsistencies. Sometimes he set critics against each other—indeed, the church was getting blasted from all sides. He offers the example of a man some say is too tall; others say too short; some say too fat; others say too lean. Maybe the man is a very odd shape, Chesterton deduces—but *"he might be the right shape."* And thus the criticisms say more about the critics.

Several generations of Christians have been emboldened by Chesterton's wisdom, among them C. S. Lewis, who borrowed some of his best arguments from *Orthodoxy* or a later Chesterton classic, *The Everlasting Man.*

Sure, some readers might say that Chesterton twisted logic to suit his purposes and he got away with it because he wrote in a personal, autobiographical style. When he couldn't nail down a point in an objective way, he just said, "I came to feel this way." But isn't that one of the paradoxes of Christianity? It can be argued rationally but it still comes down to personal testimony. And Chesterton still provided something that was desperately needed: an account of an intelligent man trusting Christ.

At a time when Christian faith was undergoing serious attacks, Chesterton countered not only with logic but also with levity. ("Angels can fly because they take themselves lightly.") That's something we should learn today.

Streams in the Desert

1925

LETTIE COWMAN

Early in the twentieth century, Charles and Lettie Cowman founded the Oriental Missionary Society. At first they worked establishing Bible training institutes in Japan and Korea. Then for five years they superintended a hundred Christian nationals who went into Japanese villages and distributed Scriptures into more than ten million homes.

But the intensity of their efforts took its toll on Charles Cowman's health. He exhausted himself in his mission work, and one day while evangelizing in Japan's mountains, he suffered a stroke that partially paralyzed his left side. The doctor told his wife Lettie, "Get him home. Your husband's work is finished."

The Cowmans returned to southern California and their hearts were heavy about leaving the mission field to which God had called them. The next years were long and pain-filled. "Often Satan came tempting us to faint under pressure," Lettie wrote, "but each time . . . God would illumine some old and familiar text or a helpful book or tract would providentially fall into our hands. . . .

"One day while walking along the seashore, almost wondering, 'Has God forgotten to be gracious?' we noticed a leaflet lying at our feet. We eagerly picked it up and found the exquisite poem, 'God smiles on His child in the eye of the storm.'"

They remembered the words of a friend, J. H. Jowett: "God does not comfort us to make us comfortable, but to make us comforters." And then Lettie seemed to hear a voice whisper to her, "Pass on to other troubled hearts some of the messages that were helpful to you throughout the years of testing."

So she began writing and compiling a daily devotional book. Much of the material is from other devotional writers whose materials were of help and comfort to Charles and Lettie. When Charles passed away, Lettie had even more impetus to help others who were going through times of testing and strain. Almost as soon as the book was published, Lettie had to have another edition printed. Edition after edition was printed, each print run larger than the one before, and some selling out within a couple of months. Published originally under the aegis of the Oriental Missionary Society, the book moved under Lettie's Cowman Publishing Company in about 1950. She died in 1960 and in 1964 Zondervan became the publisher of *Streams in the Desert.*

The total sales of *Streams in the Desert* has topped the six million mark, and even now, seventy-five years after its publication, it continues to influence lives, especially those who are struggling with difficulty as the Cowmans were.

Interestingly, the Cowmans and Oswald Chambers *(My Utmost for His Highest)* were good friends. Chambers had visited the Cowmans in Japan and later held meetings with them in England. Chambers said of Lettie, "Mrs. Cowman is a royal soul and truly a saint." And although she was an effective speaker in her own right, she preferred to use the byline Mrs. Charles E. Cowman on her books.

The Christ of the Indian Road

1925

E. STANLEY JONES

When E. Stanley Jones went as a Methodist missionary to India in 1907, little did he realize that he'd be stepping into a revolution. Oh, there was political revolution brewing as Great Britain struggled with its colonization of India, and there was some social upheaval, but that wasn't all that was changing. Jones said he never anticipated "how that revolution would not only affect Britain and India, but would affect me."

After eight years of mission work and one furlough, he felt he was a failure. And then after a life-changing experience, he decided that along with the apostle Paul he "would know nothing but Jesus Christ and him crucified before that great non-Christian world. . . . Little did I know what an adventure it would be."

Jones came to see that too much of our missionary work was merely about spreading a Western version of Christianity around the world, and not about sharing Christ. "I saw that the gospel lies in the person of Jesus Christ, that he himself is the Good News."

A Hindu lawyer once asked him, "Do you mean to say that you are not here to wipe out our civilization and replace it with your own?" That was an eye-opener for Jones. "The non-Christian almost invariably pitched the battle at the Old Testament or at Western civilization or the Christian church. I felt the heart of the matter was being left out—Jesus Christ."

In his next eight years in India, Jones did two revolutionary things: He stopped using the word *Christianity* and he explained Jesus Christ in an Indian setting.

That is the backdrop of the book. It is not an Indian interpretation of Christ, he says, but "an attempt to describe how Christ is becoming naturalized upon the Indian Road." How does the Christ of the Indian Road differ from the Christ of the Galilean Road? He answers, Not at all.

Jones's missionary heart shines through the book. "If Christianity isn't worth exporting, it isn't worth keeping." And while he was charged with being a modernist, he said it was a matter of his priorities. He wasn't as concerned about doctrine as he was about a person's relationship with Jesus Christ. "Christianity with a What emphasis is bound to be divisive." So he concentrated on the Who. "The early disciples had little ritual but a mighty Realization," he wrote. He felt that if you introduced someone to Jesus first, the doctrine would take care of itself later.

One of the biggest hindrances that missionaries had to face in India was the fact that India was a British colony. So Jones supported Indian aspirations for independence, so much so that he was banned for a time by the British authorities. While many missionaries worked with the lower castes, Jones witnessed and lectured among the intelligentsia. He said that the Kismet of Islam and the Karma of Hinduism would have to be replaced by the cross of Christ before India would see great progress as a nation.

A friend of Mahatma Gandhi, he presented a strong witness to the Indian leader. When Gandhi asked him how he had found God, Jones responded, "I didn't find God—he found me. Religions teach man's search for God, and the gospel teaches God's search for man." In his autobiography Jones states that "Gandhi was trying to find God through attainment, a disciplined attainment. I found God through obtainment—through grace." In 1961 Jones was awarded the Gandhi Peace Prize.

After *The Christ of the Indian Road,* Jones wrote many other books, but none more famous or influential than his first. In its time, it was controversial, for it questioned standard missionary procedure as well as British colonialism, but it was a key book in preparing the way for the future.

My Utmost for His Highest

1927

OSWALD CHAMBERS

There is no question that this daily devotional deserves to be on the list. It has sold millions of copies and is the best-selling daily devotional of all time. It is kept on the nightstands of Christians of all persuasions and supplies a regular stream of pithy quotes for ministers and writers around the world.

So the question is *why?* How did this book become so popular? And why is it *still* a best-seller decades after the death of its author, especially when there are so many other excellent devotionals in print?

Born in Scotland in 1874, Oswald Chambers studied to be an artist and read widely in literature, from Balzac to Ibsen. He became a Christian under the ministry of the great London preacher Charles Haddon Spurgeon. After training for the ministry, Chambers traveled internationally, speaking at conferences in Japan and the United States. After a four-year stint as principal of a Bible training college in England, he ministered to British troops in Egypt during World War I. About two years later, he took ill and died suddenly at the age of forty-three.

Though he died in 1917, it wasn't until 1924 that his wife, Biddy, began collecting material from his talks. During his life, she had taken shorthand notes of his sermons and speeches, so now it was her task to transcribe them and edit them into daily meditations. She explains in her foreword to the book that the material had been "selected from various sources, chiefly from the lectures given at the Bible Training College" and "from talks given night by night in the YMCA huts, Zeitoun, Egypt." Although Biddy's name is never mentioned in the book, she was the genius behind it.

But it was Chambers's unique personality mix that God used to make the book unique. He was an artist who read broadly. (In Egypt he said he was appropriately reading the Book of

Deuteronomy and *The Arabian Nights*.) He had a deep sense of holiness and yet he was not afraid to express himself in man-on-the-street language. ("Be godly in the grubby details.") He loathed hypocrisy and enjoyed a sense of humor. Once he put up a sign announcing his YMCA meetings: "Beware! There is a religious talk here each evening." A Scandinavian friend once said to him, "Ah, I see how you do it. You use humor and light-heartedness to plow, and then you sow the seed."

Two other classic devotionals of the day were Spurgeon's *Evening by Evening* and Tillotson's *Daily Strength for Daily Needs*. Notice the difference in the entries for May 1, for example:

> Spurgeon: "Whatever there may be of beauty in the material world, Jesus Christ possesses all that in the spiritual world in a ten-fold degree."

> Tillotson: "That which befits us, embosomed in beauty and wonder as we are, is cheerfulness, and courage, and the endeavor to realize our aspirations."

> Chambers: "Some of us always want to be illuminated saints with golden haloes and the flush of inspiration. . . . A gilt-edge saint is no good; he is abnormal, unfit for daily life. . . . We are here as men and women (not as half-fledged angels) to do the work of the world. . . . God will give us touches of inspiration when He sees we are not in danger of being led away by them. We must never make our moments of inspiration our standard; our standard is our duty."

You can see the bristling clarity in Chambers's writing, the crisp language, the touch of humor, and the practical commentary—especially compared to the other options available. Chambers ushered in a new style of devotional writing, less inspirational, more practical, aimed not so much at the emotions but at the will.

Before Biddy Chambers died in 1966, she had published sixty books, all bearing her husband's name. Of course, none of them rivaled *My Utmost for His Highest,* the best-selling devotional book of the twentieth century.

The Basis of Christian Faith

1927

FLOYD E. HAMILTON

With the subtitle *A Modern Defense of the Christian Religion,* this is one of many "defense of the faith" books published in the first half of the twentieth century. The Bible was under attack and conservative beliefs were being challenged. As a result, evangelical leaders sought to strengthen their followers through strong apologetic writings.

Several such books could be considered for inclusion on this list: James Orr's *The Faith of a Modern Christian* (1910) and Howard A. Kelly's *A Scientific Man and the Bible* (1927), as well as Wilbur M. Smith's *Therefore Stand* (1945). All of these books did much to undergird the faith of evangelicals. But we've chosen Hamilton's book because it's easy to understand, it covers all the pertinent questions, and it stayed in print for a long period of time through several editions and revisions.

Hamilton begins his preface, "During the author's first year in a state university, he passed through the experience of losing his faith in the Bible, in Jesus Christ, and in a personal God. At the end of the year there seemed little in life worth working for, and the author dropped out of college for four years, drifting aimlessly with the current of life." Then he bumped into a man who convinced him of the reasonableness of faith, inspiring Hamilton to dedicate his life to Christian service. That's what he wanted this book to do for others, to present arguments that would have been convincing to him when he was floundering as a college student.

"Christianity works," says Hamilton, and if you want to see it most clearly, "you must go to mission lands where the contrast between lives touched by Christianity and lives sunk in the depths of heathenism is most evident." The author knew firsthand of that contrast because he was serving as a missionary in Korea when he wrote the book. (After twenty years as a missionary in Korea, he returned to the United States to be general secretary of Christian education for his Orthodox Presbyterian denomination and then went back again for another tour of missionary service in Korea.)

As he looked at other books dealing with proofs of Christianity, Hamilton found that most of them (1) were too technical, (2) concentrated too much on issues that weren't vital, and (3) didn't cover "the whole field from the modern point of view." So in this book he tries to take nothing for granted. He wants to start from scratch and show that Christianity is reasonable.

He begins by establishing the validity of reason in chapter 1 and then carefully builds on it in chapters on the universe and evidences of the existence of God. He hits hard at evolution in his chapter on the origin of the world and then discusses the growth of Christianity and the other world religions.

Chapter 8 in the eighteen-chapter book is called "The Most Remarkable Book in the World." It's about the Bible, of course, and from this point on that's what Hamilton is talking about. It was important to him to establish the unity, historical trustworthiness, integrity, genuineness, and authenticity of the Bible. The only way to account for these phenomenal characteristics, he says, is supernatural inspiration. He proceeds to answer the critics' charges against Scripture, concluding with chapters on the resurrection of Christ, the fulfillment of prophecy, and Christian experience.

Throughout this century, many have accused Christians of being backward, unintelligent, duped into believing a bunch of fairy tales. Supposedly we don't care about logic or history or sense or science. But this attack should be shouted down by the sheer number of books, like Hamilton's, that have sought to establish an intellectual basis for our faith. We do care, very deeply, about what makes sense, and (as Hamilton reminds us) trusting Christ makes far more sense than not trusting Christ.

Religion That Works

1928

SAMUEL M. SHOEMAKER

Billy Graham said, "I doubt that any man in our generation has made a greater impact for God on the Christian world than did Sam Shoemaker."

He seemed forever in the middle of launching something big. Usually, after it got started, he stepped out of the way and let others take credit for it. He was a key figure in the beginnings of Alcoholics Anonymous, helping its founder adapt the small-group model for use in its Twelve Step program. And Shoemaker's *Religion That Works* has been termed "the most powerful part of the legacy bequeathed to Alcoholics Anonymous."

Shoemaker was an early leader in the Oxford Group, an international outreach movement that encouraged small groups within the church. In Pittsburgh he launched a program known as the Pittsburgh Experiment, designed to help laypeople in personal evangelism. He started the magazine *Faith at Work*, which also concerned small groups.

Longtime associate W. Irving Harris called him a "Bible Christian." The churches he served were molded into places where people could learn the how's of the faith: how to find God, how to pray, how to read the Bible, how to pass on the faith. And much of the learning of *how* emerged from fellowship in small groups.

Born in 1893, Shoemaker spent two years as a Bible teacher and evangelist with the YMCA in China before returning to America for his seminary training. Ordained an Episcopal priest in 1921, he was called to be rector of Calvary Protestant Episcopal Church in New York City in 1925 and he ministered there for the next twenty-six years.

Less than a year after he became rector, he started the Calvary Rescue Mission to reach alcoholics. It was here a few years later that the future founders of AA would be converted and later mentored by Sam Shoemaker.

Shoemaker wrote about forty books between 1923 and 1963, when he died. Many of them were collections of his Calvary Church sermons, as is *Religion That Works*. But his logical progression of thought and his clear articulation of truth make the book stand out.

"If I had but one sermon to preach," Shoemaker begins, "it would be on the homesickness of the soul for God." He went on to talk about the sin barrier and a person's need for salvation—a new birth experience. But he didn't stop at evangelism. He knew conversion had to be followed by instruction in prayer, the Scriptures, the church, the sacraments, Christian fellowship, and worship. And so his book discusses all those elements.

In his chapter "How to Know the Will of God," Shoemaker lists eight points typical of his practical wisdom: (1) pray; (2) think; (3) talk to wise people, but do not regard their decision as final; (4) beware of the decision of your own will, but do not be too much afraid of it; (5) do the next thing, for doing God's will in small things is the best preparation for knowing it in great things; (6) when decision and action are necessary, go ahead; (7) never reconsider the decision once it is finally agreed on; and (8) keep in mind that "you will probably not find out until afterward that you were led at all."

It was Shoemaker's emphasis on a religion that works that made him so successful in reaching men for Christ, whether the man was an alcoholic at the Calvary Rescue Mission or a prominent businessman in his Pittsburgh Experiment.

Who Moved the Stone?

1930

FRANK MORISON

It all started when Frank Morison (a pseudonym for journalist Albert Henry Ross) was still a teenager. It was the late 1890s, a time when modern thought was debunking Christianity and some scholars were even alleging that Jesus never existed.

Morison (we'll just call him that to avoid confusion) was caught up in the idea that the four Gospels were unreliable, and that the miracles in particular were just figments of someone's religious imagination. Fascinated by the physical sciences, young Morison accepted the logical thinking of Huxley that "miracles do not happen."

In fact Morison planned to write an essay on the seven last days of Christ's life, stripped of "its overgrowth of primitive beliefs and dogmatic suppositions." But, preoccupied with his other studies, he could not finish it.

Years later, as a full-fledged journalist, he had the opportunity to work on his essay—and now he tackled the assignment with vigor. Investigating the facts, he discovered not only that he could no longer write the book as he had once conceived it, but that he would not if he could.

Journalist Morison begins by examining the trials of Jesus Christ before the Roman and Jewish authorities, as if he were reconstructing a trial that took place five years earlier. At first suspicious of the four Gospels, he found them more credible because of the different nuances that they provided. "The broken fragments fit together and make a coherent and intelligible whole," he wrote.

So now this investigative journalist could swallow the biblical story of Christ's trial and crucifixion, but what about the resurrection? That was a miracle, and skeptics don't easily swallow miracles. Morison's book demonstrates the careful research he conducted on this miracle, with two-thirds of it examining the resurrection accounts in Scripture and looking deeply into every aspect. It's almost as if he called each biblical character onto the witness stand to tell his or her story. The surprise witness at the end of this case is the stone that covered the entry to Jesus' tomb. "Who moved the stone?" is not just Morison's title, but his main argument for the truth of the resurrection.

"Personally, I am convinced that no body of men or women could persistently and successfully have preached in Jerusalem a doctrine involving the vacancy of that tomb, without the grave itself being physically vacant. The facts were too recent; the tomb too close to that seething center of oriental life."

Did the Romans move the stone and take the body? Did the Jewish leaders have it done? Did the disciples? Morison examines the possibilities and determines that none of those options makes sense. We're left with the miraculous being the most reasonable explanation.

Morison's book has unusual power because it is not written as a theological apologetic for the resurrection, but rather as a newspaperman's inquiry. For this reason it has been convincing for many college students as well as adults who have honest questions about these pivotal truths of Christian doctrine. The book has been produced by many publishers and has been kept in print because of its effective witness. Later apologists for the Christian faith, such as Josh McDowell and Paul Little, built on Morison's foundation. And so thousands of inquiring minds have followed Morison on the logical road to the empty tomb.

Prayer

1931

OLE HALLESBY

"I have had more of a desire to write this book," Ole Hallesby writes in his preface, "than possibly any other that I have written. And yet I have been more afraid of this one than of any { 56 } other. It seems to me that it is very difficult to speak or write about prayer."

Raised in a praying family near Oslo, Norway, Hallesby had drifted away from Christianity during his early college years. At the age of twenty-three, he had a deep conversion experience that drew him back to the pietistic Lutheran faith of his parents. He became an itinerant evangelist and witnessed many religious revivals. At age thirty, he was appointed professor of dogmatic theology at the Free Faculty of Theology, and taught there from 1909 to 1952. During World War II Hallesby, one of the most outspoken church leaders against the Nazi occupation, was put under arrest for two years.

Hallesby wrote sixty-seven books in all, many of them on dogmatic theology and ethics, but he is also known for his devotional writings. His little book *Prayer,* published first in 1931, and translated into English by Clarence J. Carlsen, has sold nearly a million copies. Its simplicity is disarming. "This book does not presume to be anything more than a presentation of a few simple rules for the benefit of souls who are failing in prayer. It does not aim to give an exhaustive treatment of the great theme."

Hallesby doesn't focus on great philosophical or theological problems regarding prayer. Instead, he explains what it is and how it works, using language that any person of any ethnic group can comprehend.

To pray, he says, is nothing more than "giving Jesus access to our needs and permitting Him to exercise His own power in dealing with them." Hallesby draws on the symbolism of Revelation 3:20 ("Behold, I stand at the door, and knock") to explain prayer. "To pray is to let Jesus glorify His name in the midst of our needs."

But prayer is more than words; it is an attitude of the heart. And that attitude is characterized by helplessness and faith. "Helplessness united with faith produces prayer," he says. "Prayer consists simply in telling God day by day in what ways we feel that we are helpless." How much faith is necessary? "We have faith enough when we in our helplessness turn to Jesus." Hallesby goes on to say, "It is not intended that our faith should help Jesus to fulfill our supplications. He does not need any help; all he needs is access."

The art of prayer can be developed through practice and per-severance (which should not be onerous but delightful) and by depending on the Spirit of prayer. Near the end of the book, Hallesby discusses various problems of prayer. If God is all-knowing and all-loving, he asks, why pray? "Prayer is not for the purpose of making God good or generous. . . . Nor is it for the purpose of informing God concerning our needs. . . . No, prayer has one function, and that is to answer 'Yes' when He knocks, to open the soul and give Him the opportunity to bring us the answer." So prayer is essential for us to enjoy personal fellowship with God. Why intercessory prayer for others? Because God has chosen to transmit his power through those who open their hearts to the saving power of Jesus. "The super-natural influence of God's Spirit upon a believer's personal life results in an accession of eternal power which manifests itself in various ways in his environment and quietly but surely helps to transform this world into God's kingdom. The greatest trans-mission of power takes place through the believer's prayers and intercessions."

A Diary of Private Prayer

1936

JOHN BAILLIE

John and Donald Baillie were brothers born a year apart (1886 and 1887) in the remote Scottish Highland village of Gairloch. Both studied at Edinburgh University and later at Germany's Marburg University. Both became respected theologians as well as noted authors.

Younger brother Donald, a shy man, became professor of systematic theology at St. Andrews, where he taught for twenty years. His major work, *God Was in Christ,* is regarded as one of the classics of twentieth-century theology.

Older brother John, who was professor of divinity at Edinburgh for twenty-two years, is known in theological circles for works like *Our Knowledge of God* and *The Idea of Revelation in Modern Thought.* But his best-known work wasn't a theological tome at all. It was a simple book of prayers that ended up on the best-seller lists: *A Diary of Private Prayer.*

In a note preceding the thirty-one-day morning and evening devotional, he says simply, "Here are prayers for all the mornings and evenings of the month." Two additional morning and evening prayers are added to the end of the book in case you feel your Sunday prayers should be a bit different.

The language couched in King James English is formal, but nonetheless potent. On the morning of the ninth day his prayer opens with: "Here am I, O God, of little power and of mean estate, yet lifting up heart and voice to Thee before whom all created things are as dust and vapor."

On the evening of the twenty-seventh day, his prayer reads (in part):

> When the way seems dark before me, give me grace to walk trustingly;

When much is obscure to me, let me be all the more faithful to the little that I can clearly see;

When the distant scene is clouded, let me rejoice that at least the next step is plain;

When what Thou art is most hidden from my eyes, let me hold fast to what Thou dost command;

When insight falters, let obedience stand firm;

What I lack in faith, let me repay in love.

Each prayer comes through with poetic power, and the decades since its first publication have not diminished the book's usefulness. While the book became a best-seller in England, its sales in the United States have been strong too. It has also been translated into many other languages.

Church Dogmatics

1936

KARL BARTH

Karl Barth was no doubt the most talked about theologian of the twentieth century. He could not be ignored. Evangelicals could not agree with him; but neither could liberals. Yet both evangelicals and liberals had to deal with this celebrated neoorthodox thinker.

On the one hand, he could acknowledge that the most profound theological thought he ever had was "Jesus loves me, this I know; for the Bible tells me so." But on the other hand, he wouldn't identify Scripture as the Word of God, and his subjective approach made him hard to pin down in other significant areas.

He charged liberal theologians with neglecting great themes of Scripture like the sovereignty of God, the sinfulness of man, the wonder of God's grace, and the New Testament's emphasis on a new age in place of the notion that this world was getting better and better. And evangelicals applauded. But when he emphasized the humanity of Scripture, implying errors and questioning authorship, evangelicals started attacking.

Karl Barth, born in Basel, Switzerland, in 1886, held several Swiss pastorates before and during World War I. While he was still a pastor, he wrote his famous commentary on Romans. This book attracted attention. Barth spoke of the "theology of crisis," indicating that we had reached a turning point—in history and in Christianity. Almost overnight he became a theological celebrity, the leader of a new theological movement. Appointed professor of theology in German universities, he spoke against Adolf Hitler's rise to power. When he could not continue in German academia because of his refusal to support Nazism, he took a safer position as a professor in Basel, Switzerland, where he stayed until his retirement.

The catchphrases that he had used (either-or, Wholly Other, God is God and not man) were bandied about by young seminarians. In Europe it was recognized that liberalism had failed, and Barth was leading a revolt against it. Liberalism had domesticated God so that the Wholly Other had now become a patron saint of human values and institutions.

Church Dogmatics was published in bits and pieces beginning in 1932 (it was published in German before its release in English) and continuing through 1967. Each piece was eagerly picked up by clergy around the world as if it were a best-seller. When complete (although Barth died before he could finish his Doctrine of Reconciliation), it was a massive series of volumes containing thousands of pages.

Central in Barth's theology is the Word of God, which he says we encounter through the incarnate Word, the Word of Scripture and the Word of proclamation. He also speaks of the inability of man to come to the knowledge of God because God is Wholly Other. Some liberal theologians had talked about the spark of divinity in man, but Barth's view is that genuine humanity is found only in Jesus Christ, and in him we can speak of the humanity of God. One of his favorite verses to quote is Leviticus 26:12—"I will walk among you, and will be your God, and ye shall be my people."

To many evangelicals, Barth was anathema because of his subjectivity. What actually happened in history wasn't important to him; his emphasis on the eternal now made it seem as if biblical facts were irrelevant. All that matters, he said, is the current revelatory moment. Of course that didn't sit well with evangelicals who were fighting for the objective truth of Scripture. Yet in other ways, Barth was one of the evangelicals' greatest allies in the fight against liberalism.

There have been many noteworthy theologians in the twentieth century. Many liberal thinkers like Tillich, Bultmann, and Kung have written extensively, but none of them have had the impact, especially on conservative thought, of Karl Barth and his *Church Dogmatics*.

Worship

1936

EVELYN UNDERHILL

Besides *Worship*, at least two other books by Evelyn Underhill deserve consideration as we compile our list. Both her pioneering study *Mysticism* (1911) and her smaller work *Practical Mysticism* (1914), in which she relates her subject to the spiritual development of ordinary men and women, would be worthy candidates.

But the spiritual development of Evelyn Underhill is a fascinating study in itself. Born in 1875 into an irreligious upper-class British family, she was educated well and pursued her interests in botany, archaeology, languages, and the social sciences. As a teenager, she wrote, "As for religion, I don't quite know. . . . I think it better to love and help the poor people round me than to go on saying that I love an abstract Spirit whom I have never seen. . . . If we are to see God at all it must be through nature and our fellow men."

She married when she was thirty-two, at a time when she was becoming interested in mysticism and exploring the idea of becoming a Catholic, probably because so many medieval mystics were Catholics. However, her husband was an Anglican, and so she decided not to leave the Church of England. After she wrote her first major theological work, *Mysticism,* a Roman Catholic philosopher and mystic took her under his wing and urged her not to neglect the person of Jesus Christ and the New Testament. Following his advice, she became increasingly orthodox theologically.

The mysticism that she taught was not derived from Eastern religions, nor was it monastic (as in Catholicism). Its goal was not a selfish peace of mind but rather a spiritual union with Christ, who is the Christian's only source of inner peace.

Underhill was increasingly in demand as a spiritual director and retreat leader. She prayed an hour each day and sought to "practice the presence of Christ" as taught by Brother Lawrence. But she also visited the poor in London three times a week and helped both university professors and cleaning women develop a deeper relationship with God. Thus her writings on mysticism as well as her example broke new ground in the Protestant understanding of the subject.

Yet her book *Worship,* written when she was sixty-one, is even more significant. The *Times (London) Literary Supplement* commented, "Miss Underhill has written a masterpiece of the spiritual life, free from all professional partisanship."

In the book she presents the characteristics of Christian worship, which she calls, "the response of the creature to the Eternal . . . an acknowledgment of Transcendence, . . . of our total dependence on the free action of God." But Christian worship understands the incarnation as well, "the self-giving of the Absolute God."

After defining and discussing worship in general terms, Underhill delves into various types of worship: Jewish worship, early Christian worship, Catholic worship, Reformed worship, Free Church worship, and Anglican worship. In her presentation, she does not attempt to be analytical, but merely to explain what they try to do. Or as she puts it, her emphasis is on "the shelter they can offer to many different kinds of adoring souls, not on the shabby hassocks, the crude pictures, or the paper flowers."

Evelyn Underhill's writings on mysticism predated the emphasis on meditation in the 1960s by thirty years, and her classic work on worship also presaged the rediscovery of that subject in many Protestant churches by a half century. Many modern writers on both subjects have borrowed broadly from her seminal ideas.

The Cost of Discipleship

1937 (English, 1948)

DIETRICH BONHOEFFER

Dietrich Bonhoeffer practiced what he preached. He fought what he taught. He wrought what he wrote. Few of the century's thinkers had the opportunity to test out their ideas the way Bonhoeffer did. Few writers have ever embodied their writings to such an extent.

You could say that Dietrich Bonhoeffer was born to be a theologian. With highly educated parents and an impressive pedigree of theologians, church historians, and chaplains (along with a few political subversives), young Dietrich decided at age fourteen to enter this field. He studied at Tubingen and Berlin Universities, and later Union Theological Seminary in New York. He returned to Germany to teach at Berlin University.

Bonhoeffer's first book, *The Communion of Saints,* already shows some of the themes that would make his mark on the world, especially the responsibility of the church to judge the structures of society. Early on, he recognized the danger of Adolf Hitler's rise. When Hitler began grabbing power over the churches, Bonhoeffer quit his teaching post in protest. After two years teaching in England, he came back to his homeland and helped to establish a new "Confessing Church" (which refused to go along with Hitler) and an underground seminary.

During this time, he published *The Cost of Discipleship.* In the introduction he sets out his questions: "What did Jesus mean to say to us? What is his will for us today? How can he help us to be good Christians in the modern world?" He wants to get behind the "slogans and catchwords of ecclesiastical controversy" and hear the true challenge of Christ. "The real trouble is that the pure word of Jesus has been overlaid with so much human ballast—burdensome rules and regulations, false hopes and consolations—that it has become extremely difficult to make a genuine decision for Christ."

And so Bonhoeffer opens up the Gospels to see what Jesus says. The bulk of the book is commentary on the Sermon on the Mount (Matthew 5–7), with another section on Jesus' charge to his disciples (Matthew 10). His exposition is creative and courageous, with no attempt to sugarcoat Jesus' hard sayings.

But the enduring concept of *The Cost of Discipleship* hits the reader in the first sentence and undergirds the rest of the book. "Cheap grace is the deadly enemy of our Church," Bonhoeffer begins. "We are fighting today for costly grace." He waxes eloquent on the subject, characterizing cheap grace as a less committed Christianity, "the justification of sin without the justification of the sinner." At first blush it might seem that Bonhoeffer is pushing a salvation through works, and that is a danger here, but he slices the issue finely. Costly grace is the opportunity to follow Jesus, to do whatever it takes to please him, to suffer if necessary, perhaps even to die.

"When Christ calls a man," Bonhoeffer said in an oft-quoted axiom, "he bids him come and die." In this book he defines discipleship as a dying to self, but the further events of Bonhoeffer's life give this saying an eerie relevance.

In spite of his natural pacifism, Bonhoeffer became convinced that Hitler's evil had to be opposed. This was a struggle for him—he wasn't sure he was doing the right thing. Though friends got him out of Germany in 1939, he returned once again to join the resistance. He actively participated in a plot to overthrow Hitler, even serving as a secret liaison with the British government. Arrested by the Gestapo in 1943, he continued to write, pray, and witness in prison until his execution on April 9, 1945, just a few days before the Allies liberated the concentration camp where he was held.

That's a sad tale, and the world lost a great champion of justice, but Bonhoeffer's death was a fitting culmination to a life of costly discipleship. His total commitment gave credence to his message, and many believers have been inspired by his works as well as his words.

The Witness

1937

GRACE LIVINGSTON HILL

Maybe Grace Livingston Hill doesn't rank up there with Steinbeck and Hemingway as a great American novelist, but few would deny that the ten million novels she sold during the century did not have an impact on American Christians. Few American writers have sold more books than she did, and more of her books have been reprinted than books by Dickens, Scott, or even Zane Grey.

Her first novel was written in 1903 when she was thirty-eight and she continued writing until her death in 1947. All told, she wrote about eighty novels. Between her sixty-fifth birthday and her eightieth birthday she wrote forty-three novels, about three per year. When she died at the age of eighty-two, a half-finished novel was on her desk.

"I am not writing just for the sake of writing," she said. "I have attempted to convey through my novels a message which God has given me." Her writing technique was hardly orthodox. In *The Writer* magazine, she explained, "The truth is . . . I have no method at all. . . . I just sit down at my typewriter and go ahead. Sometimes a sentence just pops into my head and that starts me off. . . . Until the book is finished, I have no idea how the story is going to be worked out myself."

Critics often blasted her novels. The *Saturday Review of Literature* said of one of them: "A singularly sentimental and pious tract, clumsily written, fatuous, and illogical. To be candid, the book is awful." But the scathing reviews did not hurt her sales.

Her philosophy was simple: "I feel that there is enough sadness and sorrow in the world, so I try to end all my books as beautifully as possible."

But life wasn't always beautiful, even for Grace Livingston Hill. Her first marriage to Rev. Frank Hill lasted only seven years; he died from an infection after an appendectomy. Her second marriage to a church organist, Flavius Lutz, was a disaster. His tirades, tantrums, and irrational behavior made life extremely difficult. Eventually he walked out. Grace never made much of an effort to look for him but she never knew when he might return.

Grace didn't want to dwell on the hardships of life, nor did America in the dark days of World War I and the Great Depression of the 1930s. Christians were also wearied by the modernist-fundamentalist controversies, and Grace provided a retreat from those.

But Grace didn't retreat personally. When she felt that the biblical instruction she was getting in her local church was inadequate, she rented a meeting hall and invited outstanding Bible teachers to come to her town to speak. Soon a community Bible class was developed, and she sponsored it for at least fifteen years. She also started a mission Sunday school among Italian immigrants outside of town, which developed into a solid Presbyterian church.

So it was not surprising, when she sat down at her typewriter in early 1937 and began to write *The Witness,* that the hero of the novel purchases and renovates an abandoned old church.

The novel's hero, Paul Courtland, is injured in a theater fire that takes the life of his best friend. In the hospital, he recognizes a Presence with him, the Christ that his best friend knew. As he follows that Presence, his life takes on new meaning. His girlfriend, however, cannot understand the change in him, and he has to make a choice between her and Christ. He chooses to continue following the Presence. Near the end of the book he comes across that old church, in danger of being sold to an iron foundry. But, just like his author, Paul Courtland buys it and begins a ministry to the poor people of that community.

Known for her novels of romance and idealism, Grace Livingston Hill was always more interested in pointing her readers toward wholesome family relationships and solid Christian values than in producing fine works of literature. In the first half of the twentieth century, evangelical Christianity had no novelist to compare with her.

If

1938

AMY CARMICHAEL

When Amy Carmichael was twenty-six, she left her native Northern Ireland and ventured to Japan as a missionary. She lasted one year; poor health forced her to return.

The following year she went overseas again, this time to South India, sponsored by the Church of England Zenana Missionary Society. This time she lasted fifty-six years, until her death in 1951 at the age of eighty-four.

In South India she was moved by the temple slavery of little girls; in the name of religion small children were forced into prostitution. She rescued one child after another from it, and in 1925 began the Dohnavur Fellowship, an independent work dedicated to saving children in moral danger, training them to serve others, helping the desolate and the suffering, doing anything that might make God's love known, especially to the people of India. Eventually, Dohnavur sheltered some nine hundred endangered boys and girls.

When Amy was sixty-four, she fell, breaking a leg and twisting her spine. For the rest of her life, her world was the room she called the Room of Peace, her bedroom and study. Even as the apostle Paul had used his prison cell in Rome to be his site to write some of his great epistles, so Amy Carmichael began writing in her "prison cell."

Although she had written a number of books in earlier days, the first book she completed after her accident was *Gold Cord*, the story of Dohnavur Fellowship, with poems by the author beginning each chapter. After that, she wrote thirteen more books, many of them carrying some of her poetry or nugget sentences. Perhaps the best-seller of her works, and the book with the greatest impact, is the little book *If*.

She tells how the book came to be written: "A fellow worker brought me a trouble about a younger one who was missing the way of Love. This led to a wakeful night. . . . And then sentence by sentence the Ifs came, almost as if spoken aloud to the inward ear."

She wrote the book that night, shared it with others the next day, and then printed it on a hand press and bound it in booklet form.

If has three sections. The introductory section leads readers to the verse "that ye, being rooted and grounded in love, may be able to comprehend with all saints what is the breadth, and length, and depth, and height; and to know the love of Christ, which passeth knowledge" (Eph. 3:17–19). The second section, the core of the book, contains sixty-five provocative "if" statements, like these:

> If I can write an unkind letter, speak an unkind word, think an unkind thought without grief and shame, then I know nothing of Calvary love. . . .
> If I have not the patience of my Saviour with souls who grow slowly; if I know little of travail (a sharp and painful thing) till Christ be fully formed in them, then I know nothing of Calvary love.

A short third section closes with the author asking, "Lord, what is love?" and then receiving the response, "Love is that which inspired My life, and led Me to My cross, and held Me on My cross. Love is that which will make it thy joy to lay down thy life for thy brethren."

Amy Carmichael told readers that the little book was not meant to be read one page after another, but rather slowly and pensively, a little at a time. Elisabeth Elliot, who wrote Carmichael's biography, *A Chance to Die,* says that this book showed her "the shape of godliness," adding, "It was from the pages of this thin blue book that I, a teenager, began to understand the great message of the Cross, of what the author called 'Calvary love.'"

For Elliott, as for so many others, *If* was a starting point.

The Mind of the Maker

1941

DOROTHY L. SAYERS

Dorothy Sayers was a maker. Her output of high-quality literary works was enviable. Like her compatriots G. K. Chesterton and C. S. Lewis, she was accomplished in several fields.

First, she wrote detective novels. Beginning in 1921, she churned out sixteen such books, featuring her favorite sleuth, Lord Peter Wimsey. Sayers, who was also a leading scholar on the writings of Dante, provided some literary polish to a genre that often lacked it.

In 1937 she wrote a drama for the prestigious Canterbury Cathedral festival, *The Zeal of Thy House,* about architect William of Sens, the "maker" of that cathedral. This play contains some of the ideas that later emerged in *The Mind of the Maker.* (By the way, T. S. Eliot also wrote *Murder in the Cathedral* for the Canterbury festival.)

When the BBC asked her to write a series of radio plays about Jesus, Sayers responded with *The Man Born to Be King,* probably her best-known religious work. In a bold move, she chose to make Judas Iscariot the "tragic hero" of the story. Jesus, of course, couldn't have the "tragic flaw" necessary for a classic tragedy, but what if Judas's sense of pride caused his downfall—and the death of Jesus? That choice made this familiar story come alive for BBC listeners in 1941 and 1942.

Like Chesterton and Lewis, Dorothy Sayers was also a keen defender of the faith. She would write essays and letters explaining and upholding the classic Christian creeds. In fact *The Mind of the Maker* was intended as an explanation of the Trinity, as set forth in the Apostles', Nicene, and Athanasian Creeds. But it ends up being much, much more. It's a peek at the process of creating, a glimpse at the image of God, a bit of insight into what God must go through.

When the Bible says we're made in the image of God, Sayers wonders, what does that mean? All we know of God by the twenty-sixth verse of Genesis 1 is that he's a creator. So maybe we're made to be creators too.

Then she starts jamming on a subject she knows well—*making*. In her case, she makes writing. The writing process has three parts: the Idea, the Energy (that is, the work itself), and the Power (the involvement of the reader). If you're thinking Trinity, you're right. The Father is the Idea, incarnated in the Energy/Son, shared by the Power of the Spirit. That scheme may not work out exactly but it's a pretty good one. Late in the book she warns against "scalene triangles"—that is, heresies in ancient or modern times that overemphasize one part of the Trinity or underemphasize another. Seen in the light of her Idea-Energy-Power plan, her critique makes a lot of sense.

Another interesting insight is the question of free will. As a novelist, she knows the importance of letting her characters make their own choices. One friend wanted her to send Lord Peter Wimsey to Antarctica on a case, but Sayers knew he wouldn't be caught dead in that cold clime. Yet Sayers also acknowledges her own power over her characters. She is ultimately in charge of her story. Writers who create characters and let them take charge, she notes, "do not, as a matter of brutal fact, usually produce very good books."

Could this help us understand that whole conflict between God's will and our will? Again, it's not a perfect analogy, but her writer's insight proves helpful.

But besides explaining some murky theological points, *The Mind of the Maker* exalts the calling of the artist, the human maker who mirrors the work of God. Writing in 1941, Sayers noted a growing gap between the church and the arts, resulting in a "spiritual isolation" for the artist. That gap kept growing in most corners of Christendom for a few decades, but it seems to be closing now. Churches are beginning to welcome the work of the makers in their midst, and Dorothy Sayers's theology of making may have had a little something to do with that.

The Robe

1942

LLOYD C. DOUGLAS

They laughed when the fifty-two-year-old Congregational minister sat down at his typewriter to write his first novel. When Lloyd Douglas finished it and submitted it for publication, publisher after publisher rejected it. Finally, he changed the title to *Magnificent Obsession* and in 1929 he got a small Chicago publisher, Willett and Clark, to print it.

As you would expect, sales were minimal at first. But then people started talking about it. In 1932 that word-of-mouth publicity pushed *Magnificent Obsession* to eighth place among fiction best-sellers for the year. Other novelists on the best-seller list that year included Pearl Buck, Ellen Glasgow, Booth Tarkington, and A. J. Cronin.

In Douglas's first novel a physician who is despondent over his wife's death meets a sculptor who says he has discovered the formula for happiness. When the sculptor picks up a Bible, the doctor responds, "If that's it, I don't care to hear about it." But the sculptor explains that the formula is found on one page of the Bible and that he has already removed it and he keeps it elsewhere.

The secret formula, the novel discloses later, is "to invest in others in secret." Interestingly, as the book became popular, people were buying Bibles and were discussing it in coffee-table discussions. Where does the Bible say that the key to happiness is to invest in others in secret?

Douglas had found that idea in the Sermon on the Mount. In fact, as Douglas wrote more novels, he found his themes for each one—until he wrote *The Robe*—in that same sermon (Matthew 5–7).

Between 1929 and 1948 Douglas wrote ten novels, each of them making it to the best-seller list and several topping that list. Six became movies, and one was the basis for a TV series in the 1950s.

Of course the novel for which he is best known is *The Robe*, published in 1942. For two years it was on the *Publishers Weekly* best-seller list, never placing lower then fifth. On its second birthday, it passed the one million mark in sales. The biggest problem the publisher had was keeping up with the demand. Because paper was scarce during the World War II years, copies had to be printed on cheaper paper.

Tracing what might have happened to Jesus' robe after the crucifixion, *The Robe* bears only a faint resemblance to *Ben Hur*, a novel written in the nineteenth century by Lew Wallace. Both books sold millions of copies, both deal with the crucifixion, and both refer to Roman soldiers. But Douglas crafted an impressive plot of his own, following characters through the Roman Empire on a journey of faith. { 73 }

Though a clergyman, Lloyd Douglas struggled with orthodox Christian doctrine. He resigned a Lutheran pulpit in Washington, D.C. because he "did not believe what he was saying." In Los Angeles his liberal views got him in trouble with the Congregational church he was pastoring and he resigned before they could fire him. Yet, in spite of all that, God has used Douglas's novels to draw many to Scripture and to investigate once again the claims of Jesus Christ.

The Screwtape Letters

1942

C. S. LEWIS

Sometimes you'll see a "one-joke" movie. The whole piece rests on one comic premise. Is that a bad thing? It depends on the joke. If it works, if the idea sustains the whole movie, it can be very funny.

In *The Screwtape Letters*, C. S. Lewis has written a "one-joke" book, but it works. There are a zillion books out there that attempt to help the reader withstand temptation. But what if we could see things from the tempter's point of view? That would certainly give us a new look at an old subject.

So goes the premise of Lewis's clever text, purportedly a collection of letters from one demon to another. A novice tempter named Wormwood gets regular advice from his "affectionate uncle," Screwtape. These thirty-one letters cover a variety of human issues: family life, work, social relationships, spiritual pride, and so on. For Lewis, hell is a bureaucracy. And throughout the book, Screwtape refers to "the Enemy," who regularly thwarts the tempters' work. ("We must never forget what is the most repellent and inexplicable trait in our Enemy; He really loves the hairless bipeds He has created.")

Lewis, an Oxford classics professor, wrote some splendid fiction (*The Chronicles of Narnia* and his sci-fi trilogy) as well as brilliant theology (*Mere Christianity, The Problem of Pain*). With *Screwtape* he combines the two forms, using his ironic fiction to convey his ideas about God and humanity. Of course, the danger of irony is that some readers might not get it. In the preface to a later edition, Lewis cites one reader who complained that "much of the advice given in these letters seemed to him not only erroneous but positively diabolical." But there's also a danger in putting words in the mouths of devils. You automatically create sharp categories of right and wrong—there's no middle ground. So Lewis's own debatable opinions get the same treatment as basics of the faith.

Still Lewis has packed plenty of spiritual wisdom in this little book. He manages to capture a certain "psychology of temptation," the ways we all get tripped up morally. In his preface he jokes that some readers assume the book was the result of "many years' study in moral and ascetic theology. They forgot that there is an equally reliable . . . way of learning how temptation works." Strangely, *The Screwtape Letters* has a ring of authenticity—obviously not from actual demonic correspondence, but from the experience of a man who has been tempted and has learned from it.

As we think about demonic forces, Lewis warns, there are "two equal and opposite errors" we can succumb to. "One is to disbelieve in their existence. The other is to believe, and to feel an excessive and unhealthy interest in them." You may be familiar with Christians who fall into that second error, attributing every sniffle to a satanic attack. This book splits the difference. While Lewis's insight helps us acknowledge and understand the temptations we face, his humor puts those devils in their place. That is, they are clearly no match for their "Enemy," the Creator who loves us.

Surprisingly, *The Screwtape Letters* received a warm welcome in the secular market, perhaps even more so than among Christians. His clever premise and whimsical style made his theology go down easily. And apparently Christians aren't the only ones who face temptation.

The Uneasy Conscience
of Modern Fundamentalism

1947

CARL F. H. HENRY

For more than a generation, conservative Christians had been on the defensive, "contending for the faith" against a phalanx of liberals. The world was just emerging from a devastating war, but the fundamentalists had been waging a war all their own. They had developed a bunker mentality and were increasingly closed in among themselves.

In several areas the liberals had preempted the issues. For instance, conservatives had lost interest in social issues because liberals were espousing the "social gospel." Soon any attempt to redeem society was met with suspicion by fundamentalists and rejected for being too close to that liberal "social gospel." In general, fundamentalists talked about separation far more than they talked about involvement. Besides that, the fundamentalists had lost the ability to be self-critical. Indeed, they were afraid to analyze themselves lest the enemy discover their weaknesses.

But in those postwar years a new breeze began to blow in fundamentalism and a new breed of conservative thinkers was starting to speak up. In the forefront was thirty-four-year-old Carl F. H. Henry. A former newspaperman, he knew the social issues as well as the theological issues. Though he was risking his future among fundamentalists, he was not afraid to speak out and criticize conservatives.

Henry merits recognition for many reasons. *Time* magazine later recognized him as "the leading theologian of the nation's growing evangelical flank." And so he was. He was also the first editor (1956–1968) of *Christianity Today,* a leading voice of American evangelicalism, as well as the author of many theological tomes, such as his six-volume magnum opus, *God, Revelation, and Authority* (1976–1983), *Frontiers in Modern Theology* (1966), and *Christian Personal Ethics* (1957). But we feel his earlier work *The Uneasy Conscience of Modern Fundamentalism* had the greatest impact on America's evangelicals.

His case was made carefully: "It is an application of, not a revolt against, fundamentals of the faith, for which I plead." Yet no matter how carefully it was worded, it was still a scathing attack on his brethren. "Fundamentalism is the modern priest and Levite, bypassing suffering humanity."

Henry told how he had asked a hundred evangelical pastors if any of them had preached a sermon on warfare, racial hatred and intolerance, labor-management relations, or even the liquor traffic in the past six months. Not one had raised a hand.

Yes, fundamentalism had revolted against the social gospel of the liberals, and rightly so, Henry said, but in the process they had also revolted against the Christian social imperative. "If the evangelical answer is in terms of religious escapism, then the salt has lost its savor."

In the previous century evangelicals had led the way in their work for social reform, but now the issue was complicated by the fact that most reform movements were in the hands of modernists or secularists. In this climate Henry dared to suggest that evangelicals "must unite with non-evangelicals for social betterment if it is to be achieved at all." He recognized that this wouldn't be easy, but it was necessary. "The battle against evil in all its forms must be pressed unsparingly."

A few years after Henry's book was published, World Vision was launched, and then came the World Relief Commission of the National Association of Evangelicals. Evangelicals were starting to grasp the message of *The Uneasy Conscience of Modern Fundamentalism.*

Carl Henry was always a thoroughgoing conservative in politics as well as in religion. Yet at the same time throughout his life, he maintained his concern to apply his faith to modern social dilemmas.

The Seven Storey Mountain

1948

THOMAS MERTON

Conversion stories seldom become best-sellers, but Thomas Merton's pilgrimage to faith isn't a typical conversion story. In a warm and witty style, he traces the first meandering thirty-three years of his life from the mountains of southern France to a Trappist monastery near Bardstown, Kentucky.

In less than a year, Merton's autobiography sold three hundred thousand copies and in a half century perhaps four million. By now it has moved into the category of "classic" and has been acclaimed as such by Catholic, Protestant, and secularist alike.

Because Trappist monks were under a rule of silence and conversation was forbidden, some thought that Merton would never be heard from again. How wrong they were! Instead, he continued to write books, more than fifty of them—meditations, poems, essays, history, and others. His book of meditations, *New Seeds of Contemplation* (1962), is another classic work. At times he became a crusader for civil rights; at other times he attacked nuclear warfare. He was certainly not the typical Trappist monk in the Gethsemani Monastery. During the 1950s and 1960s he gained a cult following. Then his explorations of the spirituality of Eastern religions led some youth to look in that direction for spiritual answers.

But it is *The Seven Storey Mountain* that has moved many malcontent atheists to begin some spiritual soul-searching and initial steps toward God. Writing in *Commonweal* magazine, Michael Garvey summarizes it this way: "Living solely for the satisfaction of his own appetites, he gradually becomes their slave. . . . He despairs of himself finally, and then God rescues him. Anyone who spends any time around Jesus knows, and on some level lives, the same story, but Merton transformed the tale of the prodigal son into a literary thriller—jazzed up, powerfully narrated, and as impossible to put down now as it must have been a half century ago."

Born in the mountains of southern France to artist parents, one from New Zealand and the other from America, Thomas Merton got his education in bits and pieces in America, France, and England. His mother died when he was six, and his father died when he was fourteen, leaving young Merton "without a home, without a family, without a country, without a father, apparently without any friends, without any interior peace or confidence or light or understanding of my own—without God, too, without God, without heaven, without grace, without anything."

Then as his life without God descended lower and lower, "He would shed into my soul enough light to see how miserable I was." He became a convert to Communism, but that lasted only a few months.

But then God's grace shone on his darkness. "It is God who gives us faith," he writes, "and no man cometh to Christ unless the Father draweth him." But Christ drew him. And he walked out of the church a new man. "All I know is that I walked in a new world. Even the ugly buildings . . . were transfigured in it, and everything was peace in these streets designed for violence and noise. Sitting outside the tiny little Childs restaurant at 111th Street, behind the dirty boxed bushes, and eating breakfast, was like sitting in the Elysian fields."

Merton went on to make another decision—to enter the Trappist monastery, where in some ways he made his own rules. His later life was controversial, and though he had an attraction to the mystic wisdom of the East, his own faith remained grounded in his personal experience of God in Christ. He died in 1968 at the age of fifty-five when he was accidentally electrocuted while visiting a Catholic monastery in Bangkok, Thailand.

In *Commonweal,* Garvey writes, "If the appeal of *The Seven Storey Mountain* were merely literary, it would be more a curiosity than a classic. It is, first and foremost, an absolutely sincere account of a man overwhelmed by grace."

Cry, the Beloved Country

1948

ALAN PATON

In a century rife with wars and rumors of wars, there was no greater miracle than that of South Africa. The outlook was bleak for the first nine decades of the 1900s. Apartheid ruled, jigsawing the nation racially. Whites held power over blacks, often unjustly, sometimes cruelly.

As recently as 1985, any observer would predict that South Africa was due for a bloodbath. Violence had torn up other African nations, and there was growing unrest among blacks and "coloreds." Whites were losing their grip on the nation. It was only a matter of time before vengeance would have its way.

The frustrating thing for American evangelicals was that this was supposedly happening in a Christian nation. Historically the Dutch and English settlers of South Africa were good church folks, and the Anglican and Reformed churches still had a strong presence there. How could such cruelty and injustice win the day?

But then a miracle happened. The miracle of forgiveness. Black leader Nelson Mandela was released from a politically motivated imprisonment, speaking mercy, not revenge. A leadership transition began. Bishop Desmond Tutu convinced black leaders to trade punishment for truth. Cruelty of the past would be wiped off the record *as long as the perpetrators came clean*. It was a stunning experiment in public policy and quite controversial. But so far it has kept the peace.

Some seeds of this political drama were sown midcentury with the publication of Alan Paton's best-seller *Cry, the Beloved Country*. Paton was a white man with a strong attachment to the black community in South Africa. He had taught in a black school for Zulus and oversaw a reformatory outside Johannesburg for ten years. (While there, it is said, he replaced barbed wire with geraniums and allowed greater freedom to the residents.) In 1946 he was on an international tour, researching penal systems, when the idea for his classic novel came to him. He wrote chapter 1 in Norway and finished the book in San Francisco. It was published first in the United States, which had its own racial problems to consider. The book struck a chord with book buyers, and soon it was made into a musical play *(Lost in the Stars)* and later a movie.

The story follows Stephen Kumalo, an old Zulu Christian minister, on a kind of pilgrimage through his "beloved" country, looking for family members who had vanished. He heads for the metropolis of Johannesburg, where he learns that his sister has become a prostitute and that his son has killed the son of a powerful white man known as a friend of blacks. Kumalo connects later with the victim's father in scenes of understanding and redemption.

"Mr. Paton has projected with extraordinary poignancy the tragedy of South Africa's blacks, shorn of their moral law by the destruction of tribal society, corrupted by oppression, crowded into squalid slums in Johannesburg, and monstrously exploited by the whites," commented Charles J. Rolo in a 1948 *Atlantic Monthly* review.

Yet Paton seemed to hold back from moral preachments. Evil is in the environment, not personified in any particular "bad guys." In fact the novel is peopled with generally good folks in bad situations. (Rolo noted that, in Kumalo, the novelist had pulled off a rare feat: "a convincing portrait of a saintly man.")

Love is the answer in this novel, but it's tough love, love that pulls a person through pain, love that unites people who have every reason to be enemies, love that forgives. Paton produced a mature response to the South African situation he knew so well. One can't help but see a bit of Rev. Stephen Kumalo in a modern figure like Desmond Tutu. And we certainly see the power of forgiving love in the recent events that have transformed that nation.

The Pursuit of God

1948

A. W. TOZER

In his book *Living with the Giants,* Warren Wiersbe calls this book "one of the best devotional books ever written by an American pastor." H. D. Merchant, who compiled *Encounter with Books: A Guide to Christian Reading,* called it "a modern classic . . . a stirring and eloquent book."

There is no question that a book by Tozer belongs on this list, but the question is whether he should be represented by this book or by *The Divine Conquest,* another classic. *Pursuit* hits hard at the frantic activity of modern evangelicals who like to substitute motion for worship. The second book, a bit more profound, reflects on the attributes of God.

Tozer himself was a complex man. He was a mystic who loved the writings of Meister Eckhart, François Fenelon, and Evelyn Underhill in a day when few evangelicals knew what a Christian mystic was. The pastor of Chicago's Southside Alliance Church from 1928 to 1959, he had strong, almost acidic, views on most things from Christian movies to new Bible translations. His denomination, the Christian and Missionary Alliance, is characterized by its zeal for reaching the unreached in distant corners of the world, whereas Tozer's burden was to attain a quiet intimacy with the Divine. Though Tozer was not a pulpit-pounder, his words were often like sledgehammers. Wiersbe says, "To listen to Tozer preach was as safe as opening the door of a blast furnace." After Tozer had been named editor of his denominational publication, *The Alliance Witness,* the periodical attracted a readership far beyond the denomination's membership.

The Pursuit of God is 128 pages of worthwhile content. Although it can be read quickly, you'd better take your time with it, because it will take a while to digest.

Tozer begins by making the record clear: "We pursue God because, and only because, He has first put an urge within us that spurs us to the pursuit." At times, he can't resist putting in some barbs: "Current evangelicalism has laid the altar and divided the sacrificial parts, but now seems satisfied to count the stones and rearrange the pieces with never a care that there is not a sign of fire upon the top of lofty Carmel."

He quotes a medieval mystical work, *The Cloud of Unknowing:* "The man who has God as his treasure has all things in One." Later in the book he introduces readers to the deep spiritual thoughts of Nicholas of Cusa. Strange stuff for an evangelical audience.

In his chapter "The Universal Presence," Tozer speaks about divine immanence, but makes sure that the reader understands that "this is not Pantheism." God dwells in his world and yet is separated from it. At times we feel that separation, and that separation makes us feel that God is no longer present. "When we sing, 'Draw Me Nearer,' we are not thinking of the nearness of place but of the nearness of relationship."

The meat of the book is in the chapters titled "The Speaking Voice," "The Gaze of the Soul," and "Restoring the Creator-Creature Relation."

In his concluding chapter, Tozer writes, "One of the great hindrances to internal peace which the Christian encounters is the common habit of dividing our lives into two areas, the sacred and the secular." We must overcome that tendency, he admonishes. As we do, it "will unify our inner lives and make everything sacred to us."

God is not playing games with us. He wants us to enjoy his presence. "Our pursuit of God is successful, just because he is forever seeking to manifest himself to us."

The Archaeology of Palestine

1949

WILLIAM FOXWELL ALBRIGHT

During the first part of the century, the Bible was going through some hard times. Higher critics were pulling it to pieces; scientists were mocking it; historians were disregarding it. Bible-believing Christians were on the defensive.

In the relatively new scientific field of archaeology, Christians found a ray of light. Some scholars like William Ramsay (*The Cities of St. Paul,* 1907, and *The Bearing of Recent Research on the Trustworthiness of the New Testament,* 1914) brought news of how archaeological findings were supporting the historicity of Luke and John. But at times the research of Christian archaeologists was suspect; and the professional world charged that they simply found what they wanted to find.

Then along came William Foxwell Albright. He had all the credentials. With a Ph.D. from Johns Hopkins and field experience at the American Schools of Oriental Research in Jerusalem, he became editor of the *Bulletin of the American Schools of Oriental Research,* a position he held for thirty-eight years. He was also appointed professor of Semitic languages at Johns Hopkins in 1929 and held that position the rest of his life. With honorary doctorates from Yale, St. Andrews, Trinity College (Dublin), Utrecht, Oslo, and Uppsala, his scholarship was impeccable and his output prodigious. He wrote more than a thousand books and articles. And when he spoke, people listened.

Over the years of his archaeological research and studies, he became more convinced, not less, of the reliability of the Scriptures. Probably more than anyone else, he was responsible for the discrediting of the very speculative Graf-Wellhausen theory of the origins of the first five books of the Old Testament. That turned liberal thinking on its head.

The capstone of his books was *The Archaeology of Palestine.* In it he traces what archaeologists had found out about Palestine from the very earliest ages through New Testament times. Though many scholars had denied that Moses could have had anything to do with the "Books of Moses," the Pentateuch, Albright wrote, "New discoveries continue to confirm the historical accuracy or the literary antiquity of detail after detail in it. . . . It is sheer hypercriticism to deny the substantially Mosaic character of the Pentateuchal tradition."

Discussing similar dating and authorship problems with the Old Testament poetic books, he said, "Modern critical scholars have been disposed to date most of it after the Exile. . . . In the light of the Ugaritic remains of Canaanite religious literature, many of the Psalms must be pushed back into early Israelite times, not later than the tenth century. There is thus no longer any reason to refuse a Davidic date for such Psalms."

Citing critical views that, "less than half a dozen books of the New Testament were written in the first century A.D., and the Gospel of St. John was written as late as the second half of the second century," Albright concluded that recent archaeological discoveries "have dealt the coup de grace to such extreme critical views."

Albright was no fundamentalist but he acknowledged there was more to be found out than even the best scientists can discover. "Though archaeology can clarify the history and geography of ancient Palestine, it cannot explain the basic miracle of Israel's faith, which remains a unique factor in world history. But archaeology can help enormously in making the miracle rationally plausible to an intelligent person whose vision is not shortened by a materialistic world view."

And as Albright was working on his manuscript, the Dead Sea Scrolls were found, further establishing the antiquity of the biblical texts.

Peace of Soul

1949

FULTON J. SHEEN

Bishop Fulton J. Sheen upset the landscape. He was the most successful TV preacher of the 1950s. Long before Ed Sullivan or *60 Minutes* began their Sunday night TV reigns, Fulton Sheen's *Life Is Worth Living* dominated the audience ratings.

But even before his TV show, this book, *Peace of Soul,* became a nationwide best-seller. Protestants as well as Catholics were buying it, and what they discovered was that they agreed with most of what the Roman Catholic bishop was writing. At times he sounded like Billy Graham.

It was a time when Protestantism and Catholicism seemed more widely separated than ever. The Pope was talking about making Mary, as the Mother of God, the co-redemptrix—a concept that made Protestants seethe. But at the same time, there was Fulton Sheen talking about man being born again: "The soul is dead when it has not that higher life which God alone can give." Then he refers to Paul's conversion and quotes from Pascal, Thompson's classic poem "Hound of Heaven," Augustine's *Confessions,* and the story of the prodigal son. "In other religions, one must be purified before he can knock at the door; in Christianity, one knocks on the door as a sinner, and He who answers to us heals. The moral crisis is ended when Christ confronts the soul, not as law, but as Mercy, and when the soul accepts the invitation, 'Come unto me, all you that labor, and are burdened, and I will refresh you' (Matt. 11:28)."

Sheen concludes the chapter with an invitation: "What better time than now, with souls all unwashed, to come to His purifying hands? He alone is our way. Flee Him, and we are lost. He alone is our light. Depart from it, and we are blind. He alone is life. Leave Him, and we must die. . . . You say you are depressed and low in spirits? He brought you low only to make you want His heights!"

In *Peace of Soul,* Bishop Sheen targets Americans who were running to psychology for their answers. He asks readers to stop blaming their subconscious for their ills, to turn away from the psychoanalyst and turn to God, who alone can forgive our sins. Peace of soul, he said, cannot come from human sources but only through divine help.

Through the book Bishop Sheen reached several different audiences. He effectively talked to secular people with his chapters on frustration, anxiety, the denial of guilt, psychoanalysis, repression, and self-expression; and he told them that God is the answer. He also spoke effectively to Roman Catholics who were clearing away incrustations of tradition, helping them see the core of their faith. To Roman Catholic clergy his direct preaching and writing style pointed the way to effective communication with the masses. And to Protestants he showed the many similarities of his faith with theirs, and also the common foe that both Catholics and Protestants together faced in an increasingly secularized society.

Sometimes Bishop Sheen's evangelistic fervor came through so strongly that some Protestants wondered if he was truly a Catholic. But his Catholic ties remained in place.

From 1926 to 1950 he taught philosophy at the Catholic University of America. In 1950 he became national director of the Society for the Propagation of the Faith and in 1956 bishop of Rochester. During Vatican II he served on the Commission on the Missions. He spoke in almost every major city in the United States and wrote more than thirty books. But the book through which Bishop Sheen made his mark on the century was *Peace of Soul.*

Here I Stand:
A Life of Martin Luther

1950

ROLAND H. BAINTON

"On a sultry day in July in the year 1505 a lonely traveler was trudging over a parched road on the outskirts of the Saxon village of Stotternheim." Thus begins Roland Bainton's biography of the great reformer Martin Luther.

Partly because of this book, Bainton became the most influential church historian of his day. Because he combined sound scholarship with readable clarity, *Here I Stand* sold more than a million copies, an unprecedented total for a biography of an historical figure, let alone a Protestant reformer.

Many other biographies of Luther had been written previously, and new ones have been written since, and Luther has been seen on Broadway and in the movies, but Bainton's picture of the man stands tall among all the competition. *Time* magazine called this "the most readable Luther biography in English." The *New York Times* called it "excellent and eloquent." The *Chicago Tribune* said it was "sound and well-rounded."

Here I Stand also established a standard for future Christian biographies: well-researched, readable, and honest. Many biographies have been written as though they were nominating their subject for sainthood. Bainton's picture of Luther lets you admire the man as you see his humanity.

Bainton himself was born in England and came with his family to Canada in 1896 when he was only two years old. After getting his Ph.D. from Yale, he became a specialist in Reformation history. Besides his work as a professor at Yale, he wrote several other notable works, including *The Church of Our Fathers* (1941), which also sold a million copies; *The Reformation of the Sixteenth Century* (1952); and his three-volume *Women of the Reformation* (1971–1977).

But in *Here I Stand* Bainton shines through as an historical biographer. He uses enough of Luther's quotations to give you the feel of the man: "I could use two secretaries," Luther wrote in 1516. "I do almost nothing during the day but write letters. I am a conventual preacher, reader at meals, parochial preacher, director of studies, overseer of eleven monasteries, superintendent of the fish pond at Lizkau, referee of the squabble at Torgau, lecturer on Paul, collector of material for a commentary on the Psalms, and then, as I said, I am overwhelmed with letters. I rarely have full time for the canonical hours and for saying mass, not to mention my own temptations with the world, the flesh, and the Devil. You see how lazy I am."

Bainton dramatizes the historic confrontation at the Diet of Worms this way: "Here was Charles, heir of a long line of Catholic sovereigns—of Maximilian the romantic, of Ferdinand the Catholic, of Isabella the orthodox . . . ruling over a vaster domain than any save Charlemagne . . . and here before him a simple monk, a miner's son, with nothing to sustain him save his own faith in the Word of God. . . . He was well aware that he had not been reared as the son of Pharaoh's daughter, but what overpowered him was not so much that he stood in the presence of the emperor as this, that he and the emperor alike were called upon to answer before Almighty God."

Bainton tells of Luther's struggle in translating the Bible into German. When he had to describe the sacrifices of Leviticus, Luther went to the slaughterhouse and asked the butcher for the names of the inward parts of goats and bullocks. And Luther didn't know if the average German would understand the salutation to Mary: "Hail, Mary, full of grace." Luther commented that the average German would understand a "purse full of gold or a keg full of beer but what is he to make of a girl full of grace?"

He also tells the touching story of Martin at the meal table reading the story of Abraham who was told by God to sacrifice his son Isaac. When he finished reading the story, his wife, Katie, spoke up: "I do not believe it. God would not have treated his son like that."

"But, Katie," answered Luther, "he did."

The Chronicles of Narnia

1950

C. S. LEWIS

As far as we know, no one has yet uncovered the hole down which Alice slid to begin her adventures in Lewis Carroll's *Alice's Adventures in Wonderland*. If someone has, it, of course, hasn't been shipped to America.

But the wardrobe of C. S. Lewis's *The Lion, the Witch, and the Wardrobe,* the first book in the Narnia series, is alive and well and living at Wheaton (Illinois) College. Well, at least C. S. Lewis's wardrobe is there, and that is the one that reputedly got his classic children's series off to a good imaginative start.

At the beginning of the series, four children enter the world of Narnia, which is held in the wintry grip of the White Witch. They meet several denizens of this strange land—Mr. Tummus the Faun, Mr. and Mrs. Beaver, and eventually Aslan the lion. Aslan, we learn, is not a tame lion, but he's good. And powerful. When the White Witch captures one of the children, Aslan takes his place and is put to death at the Stone Table. We don't mean to spoil the story for you, but Aslan comes back to life to set Narnia free from its evil queen.

The Witch knew the Deep Magic that killed him, Aslan explains, "but there is a magic deeper still which she did not know. Her knowledge goes back only to the dawn of Time. But if she could have looked a little further back . . . she would have known that when a willing victim who had committed no treachery was killed in a traitor's stead, the Table would crack and Death itself would start working backwards."

You don't have to be a literary scholar to see the imagery here. This is the story of our lives. Aslan is a Christ-figure, rescuing us from the grip of evil, dying in our place. And he rises from the dead. Yet the success of the Narnia Chronicles is in the integrity of its world. Lewis has created a place with its own character—not just a canvas for theology to be painted on. Thousands of children (and some adults) have read these books without thinking of Christ or salvation. They just love Aslan the lion. Still, they're learning about good and evil and sacrifice and loyalty and temptation and many other themes that are strong enough on their own merits. That's why these books have been so popular with families of all religious persuasions—and of no religion at all. Some would call Lewis's work *pre-evangelism,* giving people a grid so they can understand the story of Jesus when they hear it.

Like *The Lion, the Witch, and the Wardrobe,* the other books in the Narnia series have Christian parallels but they're also exciting stories. A literature professor at Oxford, and later Cambridge, Lewis was quite interested in myth. Are there basic stories from various cultures that communicate the core truths of God and humanity? Lewis would say yes. Can we create new stories—modern myths—that do that? Absolutely, and Narnia is exhibit A. Exhibit B is Middle Earth, the mythic world of Lewis's friend J. R. R. Tolkien in *The Hobbit* and *The Lord of the Rings.* But Tolkien's work is sprawling. By comparison, Lewis's is simple. In this series, Lewis never forgot that he was writing for children, and generations of young readers are grateful.

A Man Called Peter

1951

CATHERINE MARSHALL

Many books are written after the death of a loved one. Sometimes it's the death of a child, sometimes the death of a parent, sometimes the death of a spouse. Most such books are never published and most of the ones that are published have minimal sales outside of the immediate family circle.

A Man Called Peter was different for many reasons. The subject was Peter Marshall, the celebrated chaplain of the United States Senate, whose life was suddenly cut short at the age of forty-seven. The author was his widow, Catherine Marshall, and this book launched her writing career, with numerous bestsellers to follow. A year before this biography was published, a book of Marshall's sermons, edited by Catherine, was issued under the title *Mr. Jones, Meet the Master*. Its amazing sales surpassed the one million mark. So when Catherine wrote the biography, she tucked in six of Peter's sermons at the end.

Not only did *A Man Called Peter* break into the best-seller ranks, but a few years later was turned into a Hollywood movie by Twentieth Century-Fox, and it has enjoyed numerous airings in the following decades as a TV rerun.

Peter Marshall had come to America from his native Scotland when he was twenty-five. He never lost his Scottish brogue and that added to his charm as a speaker. Four years later he had completed seminary and was ordained to the Presbyterian ministry.

Catherine met Peter when he was a thirty-one-year-old bachelor-pastor of Atlanta's Westminster Presbyterian Church and she was a twenty-year-old coed at Agnes Scott College in the city. Two years later they married, and weeks later they were moving to Washington, D.C., where Peter became pastor of the prestigious New York Avenue Church.

Adjustment to marriage was not easy for either of them. "No two lives are fused into perfect oneness without a certain amount of painful adjustment," Catherine wrote. "Every couple has difficulties."

In 1947 Peter was chosen to be chaplain of the U.S. Senate, and his prayers before that body soon became renowned. One day he prayed, "We confess, our Father, that we know we need Thee, yet our swelled heads and our stubborn wills keep us trying to do without Thee. Forgive us for making so many mountains out of molehills and for exaggerating both our own importance and the problems that confront us."

Early in January 1949 Peter was stricken with a fatal heart attack, leaving his thirty-four-year-old widow, Catherine, and their young son, Peter John, barely nine years old.

Catherine had always wanted to be a writer but she had put her ambitions on hold when she and Peter were married. Then after reading Hannah Whitall Smith's *The Christian's Secret of a Happy Life,* she received some spiritual insight and a new impetus to write.

Not only was it therapeutic to write Peter's biography, but it also set the stage for the remainder of Catherine's life. To support herself and their son, she continued to write, becoming a successful author of Christian books such as *To Live Again, Something More, Meeting God at Every Turn,* and *The Helper.* She also tried her hand at fiction, writing the beloved novel *Christy.* In time, she became one of the most popular Christian writers of the twentieth century.

In 1959 she married Leonard LeSourd, and together with John and Elizabeth Sherrill they established Chosen Books, a publishing venture that produced several best-sellers of the 1970s. Catherine Marshall died in 1983 at the age of sixty-eight.

Christ and Culture

1951

H. RICHARD NIEBUHR

The Niebuhr brothers, Richard and Reinhold, born two years apart in Wright City, Missouri, were both noted neoorthodox theologians. Although evangelicals found much to argue with in Niebuhrian theology, they cheered when the Niebuhrs started talking about sin. The Niebuhrs felt that the old liberalism was neither biblical nor logical when it soft-pedaled the scriptural teaching about the pervasiveness of sin.

While the Niebuhrs drew much from Karl Barth's thinking and thus were solidly in the neoorthodox school, they developed an American neoorthodoxy that had more social awareness than their European counterparts had.

Reinhold was more of an activist than Richard. Reinhold advocated a form of socialism and ran for office on the socialist ticket. A founding member of the Americans for Democratic Action, he was a pacifist. But when Hitler rose up in Nazi Germany, he switched his views and told Protestants to support military intervention. The goal of Christianity in society is not love as much as it is justice, because of the reality of sin and evil in the world.

Richard had different passions. In his writings he often emphasized the communal dimension of Christian living. He also attacked the major denominations for their failure to challenge trends in American society and called for more prophetic voices to speak truth to the world.

But his best-known book, and the book that has influenced evangelicals as well as neoorthodox and liberal scholars, is *Christ and Culture,* a classic work about how the church interacts with society.

Niebuhr points out five different ways in which the Christian church has confronted culture:

1. *Christ against Culture.* In this approach Christians try to divorce themselves from the world entirely. The Amish might be an example.
2. *The Christ of Culture.* In this approach Christians identify the faith with aspects of their environment.
3. *Christ above Culture.* In this approach, Christians try to form a synthesis between eternal values and certain areas of society.
4. *Christ and Culture in Paradox.* In this approach Christians may be active in the world but have little hope of accomplishing anything in it.
5. *Christ the Transformer of Culture.* In this approach Christians try to shape the world to conform to the norms of Scripture and Christian tradition. It is this approach with which he sympathizes most.

In different eras Christians have approached society in all these different ways. Sometimes they've had different approaches in the same era. For instance, in Reformation times, John Calvin worked in the city of Geneva to transform culture, following approach 5, while the Anabaptists shunned the world, following approach 1, and Martin Luther was somewhere in the middle.

Niebuhr called on Christians to understand the various approaches and appreciate the backgrounds from which they had been developed. He also challenged believers to think through their approaches, so they could work within society in a biblical manner, not just reacting to their culture in a knee-jerk way.

Christ and Culture has been foundational reading for scholars and other observers trying to make sense of Christianity in the United States over the last century. We've gone from Triumphalism early in the century, to withdrawal, to a quiescent civil religion, to militant involvement, to selective detachment, and back again.

In the 1980s another book on the same general subject had a substantial impact on Christian thinking—*The Naked Public Square: Religion and Democracy in America* by the Lutheran theologian Richard John Neuhaus (1984). Neuhaus wrote after the rise of the Moral Majority in America, and Niebuhr wrote before, but both are well worth reading.

Mere Christianity

1952

C. S. LEWIS

When Chuck Colson was beginning to look into Christianity, a friend gave him a book to help him along. The friend knew that Colson, the tough lawyer of the Nixon White House, wouldn't be an easy sell. Any false argument would be swiftly rejected. But it was this book, along with the Bible and the witness of this friend, that ushered Colson into the Kingdom. The book was *Mere Christianity*.

That story could be repeated many times. Numerous Christians can trace their conversion to an encounter with C. S. Lewis's masterpiece. If we had to pick the single most influential Christian book of the century, it would probably be this one. In our little library of impressive writings, this concise classic stands out.

It began as a series of radio messages Lewis did for the BBC. These talks became three separate booklets: *The Case for Christianity* (1943); *Christian Behaviour* (1943); and *Beyond Personality* (1945). The first of these is a crisp apologetic for the Christian faith, from natural law to atonement in fifty pages. The second could be seen as an exercise manual for the Christian life. The third waxes theological on the subject of the Trinity, but always in Lewis's inspiring, whimsical style. In 1952 the three booklets were gathered into a single volume.

The main opponent of Christianity at the time, in America but especially in England, was irrelevance. Society was supposedly "Christian," but it didn't make much of a difference in people's lives. Churches were busy quibbling over denominational details, and many educated people saw Christianity as a relic of a bygone era. True progress lay in a more scientific, materialistic approach to life, they felt.

Lewis, the respected Oxford don, begged to differ. Christianity, he insisted, *did* make sense; in fact it made far more sense than the materialism of its opponents. He set out to override denominational differences by establishing some basic Christian beliefs. (In his preface, he describes Christianity as "a hall out of which doors open into the several rooms." The rooms were the different denominations, but he was "merely" welcoming people into the central hall.)

But Lewis did far more than just describe this "hall," his cogent arguments practically dragged people in the front door. Novelist Anthony Burgess wrote in the *New York Times Book Review,* "Lewis is the ideal persuader for the half-convinced, for the good man who would like to be a Christian but finds his intellect getting in the way." And it's true, a hardened skeptic would resist Lewis's logic, but *Mere Christianity* has calmed the qualms of many seekers.

The book starts not with Bible quotes but with observations from everyday life. (Would-be apologists: Take note.) "Everyone has heard people quarreling," Lewis begins, going on to say that any quarrel is based on two competing notions of right and wrong. Where do these notions come from? *Voilà!* He has established the concept of "natural law." The Oxford don deftly dances on, explaining that we all have a sense of morality—which we routinely transgress. He is reversing the tragedy of Romans 1, reminding humanity of the truths of God that can be seen in the created order but are too often ignored. Only after he establishes our violation of natural law does he get into the truth of Christianity. Once he sets forth the problem, he can offer the biblical concept of atonement through Christ as an answer for the reader to consider.

Lewis's strategy is strong and his style is delightful. Pick up the book at any page and you find him saying things you've always wanted to say.

On science: "Science works by experiments. It watches how things behave. . . . But . . . whether there is anything behind the things science observes . . . this is not a scientific question."

On progress: "If you are on the wrong road, progress means doing an about-turn and walking back to the right road."

On other religions: "If you are an atheist you . . . have to believe that the main point in all the religions of the whole world is simply one huge mistake. If you are a Christian, you are free to think that all these religions, even the queerest ones, contain at least some hint of the truth."

On free will: "Free will, though it makes evil possible, is also the only thing that makes possible any love or goodness or joy worth having."

On our purpose: "God made us: invented us as a man invents an engine. A car is made to run on gasoline and it would not run properly on anything else. Now God designed the human machine to run on Himself."

And of course his classic quote on Jesus as a "great moral teacher": "A man who was merely a man and said the sort of things Jesus said would not be a great moral teacher. He would either be a lunatic—on a level with the man who says he is a poached egg—or else he would be the Devil of Hell. You must make your choice. Either this man was, and is, the Son of God: or else a madman or something worse."

A half century after C. S. Lewis was saying and writing these things, this book is still the one you reach for when a college student asks you to defend your faith, when a neighbor wonders what Christianity is all about, or when a new believer needs guidance. That is its enduring influence.

The Power of Positive Thinking

1952

NORMAN VINCENT PEALE

After the dark days of World War II, when the GIs came home, the last years of the 1940s were years of rebuilding. But the honeymoon was soon over. Wartime marriages were breaking up, young businessmen were going bankrupt, and a new war (called a "police action") in Korea threatened to be a long and disastrous venture with thousands of casualties. As the 1950s began, America was discouraged.

Seldom has an uplifting book been so sorely needed. When one came out, heralding something called "positive thinking," America eagerly grabbed hold.

Norman Vincent Peale called it "applied Christianity"; his critics called it "watered-down theology." But whatever it was, it stayed on the best-seller lists for months, influencing millions during the decades of the 1950s, '60s, and '70s. Religious historian Russell Balmer says that Peale's message "fit the tenor of the times in the middle decades of this century. It was a message of hope, optimism, and American middle-class values." Balmer also suggested that Peale is "probably directly or indirectly responsible for everything from Robert Schuller to the prosperity gospel." And from Dale Carnegie to Zig Ziglar and beyond, every time a motivational speaker takes the podium and starts stirring a crowd—there's a bit of Peale in his or her appeal.

When he wrote this book, Peale was the fifty-four-year-old pastor of New York City's Marble Collegiate Church. At first he couldn't find a publisher, but then Prentice-Hall took it. It became an overnight sensation. Before a paperback edition was printed, the book had sold two million hardcover copies. Promotionally, it was called "the greatest inspirational best-seller of our time." (By the end of the century, Peale's forty-six books had achieved sales of twenty-one million in forty-one languages.)

The book, Peale writes, "teaches positive thinking, not as a means to fame, riches or power, but as the practical application of faith to overcome defeat and accomplish worthwhile creative values in life. It teaches a hard, disciplinary way of life, but one which offers great joy to the person who achieves victory over himself and the difficult circumstances of the world."

In his New York City ministry he integrated psychology with his theology, and the book follows the same mix. It begins, "Believe in yourself! Have faith in your abilities!" Soon he quotes, "I can do all things through Christ which strengtheneth me" (Phil. 4:13). "Develop a tremendous faith in God," he says, "and that will give you a humble yet soundly realistic faith in yourself." So in one sense it's a self-help manual on personal happiness and fulfillment, but in another sense it's a guide to a positive lifestyle based on confidence in the goodness of God.

Often the chapter titles sound completely secular, but the text itself is full of references to Scripture and to prayer. His chapter "Try Prayer Power" concludes with ten very practical rules "for getting effective results from prayer." In his chapter "Prescription for Heartache," he finishes with "Read and believe the Bible. . . . Pray sincerely and with faith. Make prayer and faith the habit of your life. Learn to have real fellowship with God and with Jesus Christ." When he talks about inner peace, Peale refers to the "inner therapy of Christ," who provides forgiveness to "anyone who asks him."

Peale also founded *Guideposts* magazine (with four million subscribers during his lifetime), had a syndicated newspaper column, wrote about forty other books, and conducted a weekly radio program, in addition to his church ministry.

In a 1992 *Christianity Today* interview, a year before his death, Peale was asked to name his best and worst qualities. "I've got plenty of worst qualities," he replied. "A good quality I have is I have always loved Jesus Christ and I think he's the greatest thing that ever happened to this world."

Your God Is Too Small

1952

J. B. PHILLIPS

It's hard to say whether this smallish 140-page book would have made this list if it weren't for the fact that Phillips's *Letters to Young Churches* had come out in 1947. That able paraphrase of Paul's epistles bought Phillips an audience on both sides of the Atlantic. The paraphrase had been started in 1940 to encourage his church youth club, and Phillips continued to work on it through the dark years of World War II. After the war was over, his unique renderings of the apostle Paul's sometimes circuitous reasoning became popular, especially among young adults.

His unforgettable paraphrase of Romans 12:2, "Don't let the world around you squeeze you into its own mold," immediately caught on and replaced the often quoted: "And be not conformed to this world" of the traditional King James Version. Surprisingly, the Revised Standard Version got considerable flak even though it is a more literal translation, but Phillips seemed to get a free ride. Phillips might be considered the first of the postwar translations of the New Testament.

On the coattails of *Letters to Young Churches,* Phillips published *Your God Is Too Small,* a book title that has been quoted far more than the book has been read. Thus, even if it can be argued that the book's contents did not do much to change the twentieth century, the title did.

In his introduction, Phillips says that he is writing to "expose the inadequate conceptions of God . . . which prevent our catching a glimpse of the true God; and to suggest ways in which we can find the real God." So in the first half of the book he talks about a dozen misconceptions of God: the resident policeman, the parental hangover, the grand old man, the heavenly bosom, God-in-a-box, the managing director, the pale Galilean, and so on. While that delightful first section is frequently quoted, the second part is the meat and potatoes.

"We can never have too big a conception of God," Phillips says, "and the more scientific knowledge advances, the greater becomes our idea of His vast and complicated wisdom." Yet if we want to know God as a Person, "we have to accept His own planned focusing of Himself in a human being, Jesus Christ." This, he says, is *the* Fact of history.

How big is God? Only when someone sees "God down in the arena as a Man, suffering, tempted, sweating and agonized—finally dying a criminal's death," only when that person sees him as Paul did when he said, "The Son of God who loved *me* and gave Himself for *me*," as if the Act was for him alone, only then does a person truly see the greatness of God.

An Anglican clergyman whose main parish appointments were in Chichester and Salisbury, England, Phillips also wrote *Ring of Truth: A Translator's Testimony,* about his experiences in translating Scripture. Not as well-known was his battle with depression, and his book *The Wounded Healer,* published posthumously, is composed of letters to others who were struggling with depression (don't confuse it with Henri Nouwen's book of the same title).

But J. B. Phillips's greatest gifts to the twentieth-century church were his sweet paraphrase of God's words to us and this well-titled critique of our view of God.

The Daily Study Bible

1953

WILLIAM BARCLAY

"What William Barclay did for the New Testament," wrote Allan Galloway, "was to rescue it from the experts."

Barclay's eighteen-volume commentary, wending its way paragraph by paragraph from Matthew through Revelation, is as insightful as it is refreshing. Many New Testament commentary series have been published in the past century, and frankly some of them match Barclay's as far as exegeting the text. But Barclay had a unique way of bringing in parallels from Hebrew, Greek, and Roman culture, as well as digging into the derivation of the Greek words. That's why his commentaries have sold an unprecedented 1.5 million copies and have been translated into many languages.

His orthodoxy can be questioned on several important doctrines, and that can be disturbing, but even conservative readers buy his books. Why? Because he did such a unique job in helping the reader understand Scripture. His colleague Allan Galloway explains it this way: "He renewed the New Testament's availability to the plain man. This was done without any sacrifice of his own scholarship or scholarly standards."

A Scotsman, Barclay was ordained in the Church of Scotland and was a parish pastor for fourteen years before joining the faculty of Glasgow University, where he taught for twenty-seven years. Besides his professorial duties, he conducted the college choir, had a successful religious TV series, wrote a long-running column in the *British Weekly,* and wrote more than fifty books.

In the introduction to one of his books he says, "I am well aware that there are those . . . who will think that some of the things in it are mistaken and misguided. I can only say to them that . . . I have found the Jesus who is the Saviour of men and who is my Saviour. . . . This is what I believe, and this is how there came into my life the new relationship with God which is the very essence of the Christian faith and of the work of Jesus Christ."

Barclay began the commentary series "almost accidentally," he says. The Church of Scotland had asked him to write something on Acts, and so he did. Then they asked him to write about another New Testament book. "As these columns went on, the idea of the whole series developed. . . . The whole aim of these books is summed up in Richard of Chichester's famous prayer: They are meant to enable men and women to know Jesus Christ more clearly, to love Him more dearly, and to follow Him more nearly."

Few scholars have equaled Barclay's meticulous research into the everyday life of people in New Testament times. One scholar remarked snidely, "William Barclay? Isn't that the fellow who tells you what Jesus had for breakfast?" Well, yes. Barclay seemed to know all there was to know about the daily habits of the Jews of Jesus' day—even their menus.

His commentaries quote relevantly from a wide range of ancient and modern literature. As he talks about "adoption" in Ephesians 1, he details the Roman laws of the time. A few verses later, on deliverance and forgiveness, he quotes Seneca, Shakespeare, Aristotle, Cicero, and Plutarch.

When he expounds on the parable of the woman who lost the coin and swept her house to find it, he describes the typical Palestinian peasant's house, with only "one circular window not much more than about eighteen inches wide," and the floor covered with dried reeds and rushes. Then he gives two reasons why the woman was so eager to find the coin: perhaps due to her extreme poverty; or because "in Palestine the mark of a married woman was a head-dress made of ten silver coins linked together by a silver chain."

Jesus once said, "Every scribe who has been trained for the kingdom of heaven is like a householder who brings out of his treasure what is new and what is old" (Matt. 13:52 RSV). That's William Barclay.

New Bible Commentary

1953

F. DAVIDSON, A. M. STIBBS, *and* E. F. KEVAN

So what was the *old* Bible commentary? Our guess is the *Commentary on the Whole Bible* by Robert Jamieson, John Fausset, and David Brown, which had been the standard one-volume Bible commentary evangelicals had been using for seventy-five { 105 } years. In clergy-talk it was simply JFB (after its three authors), and ministers, scholars, and students followed it faithfully.

But a lot had happened since J, F, and B had put their thoughts on paper around 1875. The Bible hadn't changed, but the world had. And there were new linguistic and archaeological findings that shed light on Scripture. The good old JFB just wasn't good enough anymore. So shortly after World War II, three British scholars—F. Davidson, A. M. Stibbs, and E. F. Kevan—teamed up to produce a new one-volume commentary on the Bible.

Sometimes publishers see a need but they don't realize how great the need is until they start to meet it. So it was with the *New Bible Commentary*. Pastors and professors rushed to get this new resource. It was such an immediate success that a second edition, with a few revisions, was published the following year.

The main appeal of this commentary was its newness. You could still count on JFB to give you the basic meaning of a text, but the *New Bible Commentary* made its comments up-to-date in a changing world—that was still changing.

In the 1960s Inter-Varsity Fellowship decided that it was time to do a major revision of the work of the Davidson, Stibbs, and Kevan commentary. Research into the Dead Sea Scrolls provided exciting new insight on Scripture, and increasingly people were using the Revised Standard Version of the Bible. These major developments signaled a need for a major overhaul of the decade-old commentary.

So Inter-Varsity commissioned a full-scale revision, using as its chief framers Donald Guthrie of the London Bible College and Alec Motyer of St. Luke's Church, London. Two well-known consultants, A. M. Stibbs of Oak Hill Theological College in London, who worked on the original edition; and D. J. Wiseman, Assyriologist at the University of London, provided the professional backup. The result was *The New Bible Commentary Revised,* eventually published in 1970.

More than fifty contributors wrote the twelve introductory articles and the exegesis of the sixty-six books. Twenty-four of these scholars came from England and nine from the United States, with others from Canada, Australia, South Africa, New Zealand, Scotland, and Ireland.

In the preface, the general editors state their aim: "to provide for the serious student of the Bible a new and up-to-date treatment of the text which combines unqualified belief in its divine inspiration, essential historical trustworthiness and positive Christian usefulness with general scholarship." Without a doubt, they hit their target. A one-volume commentary is not the place to discuss speculative issues or even to go in depth into exegetical questions (as a commentary on a single book of Scripture might). Even so, its 1,300 pages contain nearly 1.5 million words that will continue to help pastors, teachers, and other students of Scripture to understand various texts in the Bible.

New one-volume commentaries have been published since 1970, but all of them have had to be evaluated against this one. It is readable, scholarly, applicable, insightful, and portable—as a one-volume Bible commentary should be.

Peace with God

1953

BILLY GRAHAM

It may seem strange that *peace* should have been such a compelling word a half-dozen years after World War II ended. But the United States and Russia were regularly testing bigger and bigger A-bombs, China was threatening to enter the Korean War, and Senator Joe McCarthy was talking about Communists infiltrating the country.

Bigger than the issue of obtaining peace with man, however, is the problem of obtaining peace with God.

Evangelist Billy Graham was just emerging as a major figure in American religion. His first major crusade (Los Angeles 1949) had brought him to national attention. In 1950 *Newsweek* declared that Graham had "clinched the title as America's greatest living evangelist." In 1951 *Look* magazine, in discussing the reasons for Graham's rise to fame, noted, "All the substitutes for religious faith seemed to have failed when he [Billy Graham] appeared. The scientists had to confess that though they could control the atom, they couldn't control human beings. Communism and fascism, which purchased human freedom with promises of security and happiness, gave nothing in return. The failures of these ideologies sent people searching for a personal faith"—and a personal peace.

Graham's ministry was expanding. His *Hour of Decision* radio broadcast, launched in 1950, was soon on 150 stations and he began writing a nationally syndicated newspaper column.

Often criticized because some conversions didn't seem to last, Graham began looking for ways to cement the effects of his evangelistic rallies. In a moment of high emotion a person might walk forward in a stadium, making a commitment to Christ—but would that person remember the content of the message a week later? When Doubleday asked Graham to write a book, it seemed like a good way to give new converts a tool to solidify their fragile faith.

Graham wasn't sure he could write a book, so the publisher assigned him a ghostwriter to work some of his sermons into a best-seller. Big mistake. Graham didn't like what the writer came up with, so he decided to do it himself—with help from his wife, Ruth. He also consulted with some theologian friends, including Donald Grey Barnhouse and Harold Ockenga.

The result was *Peace with God,* which summed up Graham's gospel message in book form. Biographer John Pollock writes, "For the purpose to which it was dedicated . . . [this book] has proved matchless." And what was the purpose? "To confront ordinary people, reared to different forms of Christianity or none, with the basic Christian claim, and to enable them to put their faith in the living Christ and take the first steps on the road to spiritual riches." When he began receiving letters from people around the world who made their commitment to Jesus as a result of reading the book, Graham knew it was hitting its mark.

Within three months the book sold more than 125,000 copies. In a dozen years it sold more than 1.2 million copies in English, not counting the numerous foreign language editions.

In the preface Graham states, "I am convinced that there is a great hungering and thirst of soul on the part of the average man for peace with God." In this century, no one has been better at articulating the need of his audience. The first section of *Peace with God* continues to ask the questions the readers are asking: Why do I sin? Where will I go when I die? Does God really care about me?

The second section talks about Christ, the necessity for repentance and faith, the new birth experience, and assurance of salvation—the simple gospel that Graham had been preaching all along. In the final section, he discusses enemies of the soul, the church, the future, and peace with God.

Graham went on to write many other books, usually on the best-seller lists, and to play a key role in the founding of *Christianity Today* magazine, as well as his own *Decision* magazine, but he is best known as the evangelist who has preached to more people than anyone else in Christian history. He is certainly a dominant figure in American religion in the twentieth century, and this book nicely capsulizes his career.

The Household of God

1953

LESSLIE NEWBIGIN

Lesslie Newbigin may not have thrown much weight around Christian bookstores in America, but he sure packed a wallop around the world.

When you look at his résumé, you can see why. He was bishop { 109 } of the Church of South India, general secretary of the International Missionary Council, editor of the "International Review of Missions," and an early leader in the World Council of Churches.

One authority said that he "has few if any peers in this half of the twentieth century for laying the biblical and theological foundations for missions." *Christianity Today* called him a "world-class theologian" who wrote "books without footnotes." He had a wide range of interests including missions, evangelism, ecclesiology, and apologetics. When you read one of his books, it's almost like reading C. S. Lewis because it is understandable, stimulating, and mind-stretching.

In 1936 Newbigin left his native England to become a missionary in India. When the Church of South India was formed in 1947, uniting Anglican, Methodist, Presbyterian, and Congregational churches, he became one of its first bishops. As he contemplated that union of churches, he realized that very little had been written on the doctrine of the church, except polemical books, which tried to prove that one church's polity was better than the rest. So he wrote *Rethinking the Church,* seeking to find biblical directions for the new ecumenical church of South India. About four years later, he was asked to update the book for a wider audience. The result was *The Household of God.*

The book grabbed the attention of not only the ecumenical world of Protestantism but also the Roman Catholic world. It was a book the Second Vatican Council in Rome a decade later seriously considered, and the Pope's "Light of the World" pronouncement *(Lumen Gentium)* was influenced by Newbigin's book. Beyond that, Newbigin's book was one of the first to recognize Pentecostals as a group that needed to be invited into discussions about the future church. He became one of the few theological thinkers who could speak to all poles of Christendom: the liberal, the evangelical, the charismatic, and the Catholic.

The key to effective missionary work, he said, was to raise up believing congregations. "How can this strange story of God made man, of a crucified Savior, of resurrection and new creation, become credible for those whose entire mental training has conditioned them to believe that the real world is a world that can be satisfactorily explained and managed without the hypothesis of God? I know of only one clue to the answering of that question, only one real hermeneutic of the gospel: congregations that believe it."

He was horrified by the kind of attitude among Christians that says, "Well, I happen to be a Christian, but of course I wouldn't expect you to think that." He expressed his concerns about the directions of the ecumenical movement. All religions are not equally valid. Christianity is unique because Jesus is uniquely the Son of God; he is the only Way. Religion isn't a matter of personal taste. A bold proclamation of the Bible story, especially of the life, death, and resurrection of Jesus, must make up the central authority for Christian preaching, whether the preaching is in the East or the West. It is not true, he said, that all roads lead to the peak of the same mountain. Some roads lead over the precipice. When the World Council of Churches heard Pete Seeger sing, "Pie in the sky when you die" at its 1968 Uppsala Assembly, Newbigin was deeply disturbed by the mockery of the Christian hope.

This surprising man might be traveling the dusty roads of a remote Indian village one day and then flying to Switzerland the next day to meet with the great theologians of the world. In 1952, for instance, he chaired the "Committee of Twenty-Five," a group of the world's most noted theologians, which included Karl Barth, Emil Brunner, and Reinhold Niebuhr, as they drafted a statement on Christian hope. Afterward he returned to the villages of India to resume his missionary work, strengthening the household of God.

The Christian View of Science and Scripture

1954

BERNARD RAMM

About the time of the Scopes "monkey trial" in Dayton, Tennessee, that pitted Clarence Darrow against William Jennings Bryan, there was a young boy in Butte, Montana, who was learning about science from the father of one of his playmates. The lad was Bernard Ramm, who seemed to devour subjects like atomic theory and relativity. { 111 }

After Ramm became a Christian, he decided against a career in science and chose to go to seminary instead. But he couldn't forget his interest in science. His Ph.D. dissertation was titled, "In Investigation of Some Recent Efforts to Justify Metaphysical Statements from Science with Special Reference to Physics."

Theologically, he was tempted to live his life "within the confines of a small fort with very high walls." As an evangelical scholar, that would have been the safe thing to do. His first major work, *Protestant Christian Evidences* (1953), makes the case for the inspiration of Scripture. In it he talks about fulfilled prophecy, the resurrection of Christ, and the unique character of the Bible. "Christianity stands verified by a supernatural book," he said. Evangelicals applauded.

But his next book, *The Christian View of Science and Scripture,* stirred up controversy. While the first part of the book deals with general issues regarding science and theology, the second part looks at specific sciences and the apparent conflicts that Christian scholars have had with them. Christianity, Ramm argued, must not be identified with a particular scientific worldview. Genesis 1, he says, does not defend "Aristotle or Ptolemy or Copernicus or Newton or Einstein or Milne."

In this book Ramm sought to create an approach that would harmonize scientific thinking and the Bible. After all, he said,

God wrote both the Bible and the book of nature, so they shouldn't clash. He made it clear that not all evangelicals believe that human beings were created in 4004 B.C., and that there is no problem in believing that the universe might be billions of years old. The Bible, he said, was not written as a scientific textbook, but rather as a literary vehicle to reveal the nature of God. Biblical language is popular, not scientific. Genesis, he said, is about the First Cause, while geology and modern science deal with secondary causes.

Ramm put forth several possible theories of creation, any one of which God might possibly have used, but in his opinion the theory that best fit the evidence was the theory of *progressive creationism*. This view, he explained, attributes the order of the universe to the guidance of the Holy Spirit in a succession of divine creative acts.

He urged conservative Christians not to take an antiscience attitude. Certainly many scientists have interpreted the scientific data from a naturalistic philosophy, but a Christian who takes divine creation seriously can look at the same data and see God working in it.

The book was discussed for a decade or more. Some conservative scholars felt that Ramm's view of biblical inspiration gave away too much when he implied that the Bible did not need to be accurate in scientific details. Yet others, including Billy Graham, supported him. And when the dust had settled, Bernard Ramm's book had become the standard evangelical text on the subject of science and faith.

Ramm himself continued to write and teach. Rather than making grand pronouncements, he seemed to want to prod Christians into thinking for themselves. Many feel that his greatest book was *Special Revelation and the Word of God* (1951), and Ramm himself apparently felt drawn to his *Protestant Biblical Interpretation,* which he revised three times in twenty years, but the book that changed the century was undoubtedly *The Christian View of Science and Scripture.*

The Bridges of God

1955

DONALD ANDERSON McGAVRAN

The spectacular church growth movement, which became so dominant in the latter half of the twentieth century, dates its birth to the day this book was published in 1955.

At the time it didn't seem very auspicious. The paperback book released in England by World Dominion Press and distributed in the United States by Friendship Press sold slowly at first. It didn't have a second American printing until 1968. And its author was a fifty-eight-year-old missionary to India, who had served for more than three decades in places like Jabalpur and Mungeli and had translated the Gospels into the Chattisgarhi dialect. Not exactly the stuff that characterizes most "books that changed the century."

With the subtitle *A Study in the Strategy of Missions,* McGavran wrote the book "in the hope that it will shed light on the process of how peoples become Christian, and help direct the attention of those who love the Lord to the highways of the Spirit along which his redemptive Church can advance."

He was concerned about the millions of dollars being spent on the missionary enterprise without anyone checking to see whether the stewardship was effective. "How peoples become Christian clearly needs a great deal more study," he wrote. To some, this seemed heretical. People become Christian by the preaching of the gospel and the work of the Holy Spirit, don't they? Why do we need further study? But McGavran asked, "Why does the response to the gospel vary so much from place to place?"

McGavran was particularly enamored with "people movements," in which whole tribes of people move toward Christianity. People movements become the bridges of God to win men and women to the gospel. It is hard for us in the West to understand this, he said, because we are so ingrained with individualism, but there is "a social factor which must be taken into account when people are being discipled." The author traces people movements from New Testament times to the present, and also the development of mission stations in the past century. "Christianity has flowed most powerfully when it has flowed within peoples."

McGavran carefully answers questions like "Are you concentrating on quantity of converts rather than quality?" He says that working with people movements provides both. "Aren't you making the method take precedence over the message?" "Can salvation arise through a group decision?" In this book, McGavran tries to answer these and other questions. He closes by asking for "specialists in growth" to be "trained and used as a regular part of the staff of Christian missions." At the time it must have seemed like a far-fetched dream.

But in a few years he had written *How Churches Grow* (1959), established the Institute of Church Growth in Portland, Oregon (1961), started the *Church Growth Bulletin* (1964), moved his Institute under the Fuller Theological Seminary umbrella (1965), and published a comprehensive work *Understanding Church Growth* (1970). By this time seminarians were measuring the size, number, ethnic and cultural composition, and relationship to the undiscipled—anthropological calculations—to see what could be learned about how God is working among peoples around the world.

Until about 1975 church growth largely concerned Third World countries where the bulk of missionary work was conducted. But then the principles began to be applied to churches in the United States. Despite controversy over the emphasis on methodology, many American churches, applying church growth principles, grew rapidly into megachurches.

And it all began when a thin 158-page book was published in 1955.

The Burden Is Light

1955

EUGENIA PRICE

The year was 1949. She was thirty-three years old, had her own production company in Chicago, wrote daytime soap operas and nighttime freelance shows. From all appearances, she looked as if she were doing quite well, thank you. But Genie Price knew differently.

The Burden Is Light is the story of her unlikely conversion. And what made her story special was her unique personality: "No stuffiness, no staginess, no conventionality (not even in vocabulary), just sheer joy in Christ and the infectious longing to share that joy with others," as writer Paul S. Rees described her.

After a "chance" meeting with a high school girlfriend when she was home on vacation one summer, Price traveled to New York a month later to talk to her again. Genie was very successful but bored with life. Chain-smoking and overweight, she felt she had nothing more to write and nothing meaningful to say. On the way to New York, someone gave her a copy of Thomas Merton's *The Seven Storey Mountain,* which relates his conversion from atheism. She read it but she wasn't interested in conversion.

In New York her girlfriend took her to hear Episcopal clergyman Samuel Shoemaker, who spoke of the grace of God in Jesus Christ. Back in her hotel room she picked up a Gideon Bible and was brought to tears by Ezekiel's description of the new temple. She started reading the New Testament and when she got to the Gospel of John, she was enthralled. As a fan of the phrasing of Gertrude Stein, she exclaimed, "John is better than Gertie." While the beauty of the writing of Scripture impressed her, she was most impressed with the personality of Jesus Christ. "My attention was completely taken up mentally, emotionally and spiritually by the person of Jesus Christ. . . . And the more I thought about Him, the more real He became to me; and the more real He became, the more I wanted Him to be mine. And then my simple theology came into being. He seemed to say: 'I'll be yours if you'll be mine.'"

The Burden Is Light records not only her conversion, but also the first years—difficult ones—in her Christian life. She gave up her production company and her radio writing career. Soon she was asked to write a dramatic Christian radio show, *Unshackled,* based on the conversion stories of men and women. Many of them came from the files of Chicago's historic Pacific Garden Mission on South State Street.

The story line of *The Burden Is Light* ends there, before Price's fortieth birthday. But six years later, she "discovered" St. Simons Island off the Georgia coast and was captivated by its history. Selling her Chicago home, she moved to St. Simons, where she lived with fellow writer Joyce Blackburn until Price's death in 1996. She loved the island, she said, because "God walks very naturally among these people." Her first novel about the area, *Beloved Invader,* tells the history of Christ Church in Frederica and of her hero, Anson Dodge. With that launching pad, Eugenia Price went on to become one of America's most beloved novelists of the latter part of the century.

At the time of her death in 1996, she was known as the grande dame of Southern romantic fiction, the author of thirty-nine novels, which appeared frequently on the *New York Times* bestseller lists, with aggregate sales of more than fifty million copies.

While Grace Livingston Hill amassed great sales statistics by publishing nice stories, Price was a real writer, always working to hone her craft. She developed the genre of the historical romance, which many later writers would add to. While most of her fiction sold in the secular market, there was always a Christian sensibility to it. Genie Price took her "simple theology" out to the world, shining like a light.

Second Thoughts on the Dead Sea Scrolls

1956

F. F. BRUCE

When F. F. Bruce talked, people listened. It wasn't because he was particularly clever in his writing or novel in his ideas, but when he wrote he was clear, reliable, and balanced. And that's what was needed after the Dead Sea Scrolls were found.

In 1947 a shepherd boy found in a cave some old scrolls, which turned the world of biblical scholarship on its ear. More scrolls were found and they were extensively translated and studied. This cave turned out to be some sort of library for an ancient Jewish sect known as the Essenes, in a community called Qumran, dating to about 100 B.C.

Undoubtedly the Dead Sea Scrolls were one of the greatest discoveries of the century. But what did they mean? How significant were they? Many scholars and pseudoscholars had their say. Some suggested that John the Baptist was a member of the Qumran community or that Jesus was the Teacher of Righteousness the scrolls mentioned. Others predicted the Dead Sea Scrolls would somehow debunk Christianity.

So when F. F. Bruce wrote his *Second Thoughts,* the evangelical world looked for answers it could trust. Bruce wouldn't make any extravagant claims that couldn't be backed up. He would tell it straight.

In his preface Bruce says, "As more and more information comes to hand about these documents, earlier estimates of their significance have to be revised. Indeed, the word 'second' in the title must be interpreted in a liberal sense. Some of the thoughts which find expression here are probably third, fourth, or even fifth thoughts. But they are certainly not last thoughts."

F. F. Bruce was a British New Testament scholar who taught Greek and biblical studies at Edinburgh, Leeds, Sheffield, and

Manchester. Associated with the Plymouth Brethren, he was thoroughly evangelical but he demonstrated that being an evangelical is not incompatible with honest intellectual investigation.

He was best known for his commentaries, his writings on the early church, and his books on early New Testament documents. Among his books: *Are the New Testament Documents Reliable?* and *The Books and the Parchments.* So when his *Second Thoughts* was published, evangelicals weren't looking for any startling new revelations from Qumran, but rather for someone to make sense out of it for them.

Bruce begins by telling the amazing story of the discoveries of the various finds. He quotes W. F. Albright, on seeing a few prints from the Isaiah scroll, as saying "A date around 100 B.C. ... What an absolutely incredible find!" If the dating was solid, these manuscripts were "older by at least a thousand years than any hitherto known."

His chapter on how the Dead Sea Scrolls affect our understanding of the Old Testament text is fascinating, and it's followed by a chapter analyzing how the Qumran community interpreted the Old Testament. He likens Qumran's handling of some Scriptures to the way that some modern Bible teachers have "proven" from Scripture that Hitler or Stalin was the Antichrist.

But in his last chapter, "Qumran and Christianity," Bruce points out the fallacies of those who alleged that Qumran, rather than Bethlehem, was the cradle of Christianity or that Jesus could be identified as the Teacher of Righteousness or that the Qumran community was really a Jewish Christian sect. It's possible, Bruce allows, that John the Baptist had some contact with the Essenes of Qumran, but there are so many differences in his teaching from that of Qumran. As far as Jesus having any association with them, Bruce says, "there is no flavor of Qumran about his way of life."

"Noble as the mission of the Qumran community was," Bruce comments, "that role could never be adequately filled by withdrawal from contact with sinners. The perfect Servant, when he came, was criticized because he welcomed sinners and accepted invitations to their homes. . . . If sinners are to be delivered from their sin and changed into new men and women, it must be by one whose friendship towards them is real, unaffected, and unlimited. He who was called the friend of sinners in his lifetime has been known as the friend of sinners ever since."

Through Gates of Splendor

1957

ELISABETH ELLIOT

The news shocked the nation. Five young missionaries were murdered by Ecuadorian jungle tribesmen. Early in January 1956, the five had established contact with a band of Auca Indians, but then radio contact was lost; rescue teams went in and found the bodies.

Life magazine sent its ace photographer Cornell Capa to the jungle to do a riveting cover story. *Readers Digest* sent editor Clarence Hall to do a major article. But the story that the world was waiting for was *Through Gates of Splendor,* written by Elisabeth Elliot, widow of one of the five martyrs. Published by Harper and Brothers of New York, it launched a string of popular missionary biographies by major New York publishers. It also launched Elisabeth Elliot as a major evangelical author and speaker. But more than that, it touched the hearts of readers, many of whom responded to the missionary call to give their lives in sacrificial service.

The five young men came from varied backgrounds and were sponsored by different mission boards. Elisabeth's husband, Jim, was from Oregon, a Greek major in college and a star wrestler. Pete Fleming, from Washington, had majored in literature. Ed McCully, from Wisconsin, was a business/economics major who had lettered in football and track. Philadelphian Nate Saint was the group's pilot, one of the original pilots of the Missionary Aviation Fellowship, who had learned the ins and outs of aircraft in the Air Force during World War II. Roger Youderian, raised on a ranch in Montana, became a paratrooper in Europe and was decorated for action in the Battle of the Bulge. All five were married, and their wives were stationed in South America with them.

Elisabeth Elliot weaves the story of the five men slowly and suspensefully—even though the reader knows how the story will end. Each man and each wife are carefully and empathetically drawn. Unlike some missionary stories of the past, these people are not cardboard saints. They laugh and kid and groan. Ed writes his wife: "Dearest Baby, . . . We are certainly eating well. This has been a well-fed operation from start to end." Nate scrawls in his notebook, "Except for the forty-seven billion flying insects of every sort, this place is a little paradise."

After they prayed together, these missionaries would sing a hymn, "We Rest on Thee, our Shield and our Defender." The last two lines are, "When passing through the gates of pearly splendor, victors, we rest with Thee through endless days." Elisabeth Elliot chose her title from those words.

{ 120 } It seemed at first that the Aucas were receptive to the missionary visitors. Preliminary contacts were favorable. "Looks like they'll be here for the early afternoon service," Nate radioed on that fateful day. "Will contact you next at four-thirty." But no call came at four-thirty. The five young missionaries, who had been so careful to do everything right, had been slain.

In the next twelve months, Elisabeth, a grieving widow, wrote the classic manuscript, closing with a prayer that the gospel would yet be gotten to the Aucas. "How can this be done? God, who led the five, will lead others, in his time and way."

And he did. Two years later, the author continued her missionary work by taking her infant daughter and living among the Aucas. Many of them were converted. Returning to the United States in 1963, she became well-known as a speaker and writer. Among her best-known books are *Shadow of the Almighty, The Making of a Man, A Chance to Die,* and *Passion and Purity.*

But the book's greatest impact came in the hearts and lives of readers who dedicated themselves to follow in the footsteps of these five martyrs. The missionary life had lost some luster since the colonial days of David Livingstone. But in dramatic fashion, *Through Gates of Splendor* painted a portrait of five ordinary Joes totally committed to sharing Christ with the most unlikely recipients. There would be no more Livingstones, but this book inspired an army of Jim Elliotts and Nate Saints.

The Meaning of Persons

1957

PAUL TOURNIER

There was something wise and wonderful about how Swiss psychotherapist Paul Tournier burst on the American scene in the mid-1950s.

{ 121 }

First he wrote *A Doctor's Casebook in the Light of the Bible,* which, to tell the truth, didn't "burst" on anyone's "scene," but it alerted the reading public to Tournier's presence. It was a warm and thoughtful book by a physician of profound faith who believed that a person's physical and emotional health was rooted in a wholesome spiritual life. The depth and spiritual insight made you want to read the book a second or a third time.

Then came *The Meaning of Persons.* Other books followed, but this one established Tournier as an expert and a communicator. He not only successfully integrated psychology and Christianity but told about it in such a disarming way that you felt included—not as a patient in his office, but as his friend.

Born in Geneva, Switzerland, the son of a pastor, Tournier spent his adult life (except for an army stint) as a general practitioner in private practice in Geneva. In 1932, through the Oxford movement, he gained a personal relationship with Jesus Christ, and that changed his whole perspective on psychology as well. More and more he moved into psychotherapy, realizing the need to treat his patients as whole human beings. He saw that illness could have emotional and spiritual as well as physical origins, and vice versa.

Though his professional colleagues were slow to acknowledge his approach, he gradually attained an international standing. He describes his approach briefly in a later book *The Person Reborn:* "Technology and faith work together. Psychoanalysis explores the problems in order to bring them out into the daylight, grace dissolves them." The authentic person can be relieved, reached, and helped "only through living dialogue between man and man, and man and God."

What is remarkable about Tournier is the very natural way in which he brings in the spiritual dimension and the need for a relationship with God through Jesus Christ. "The true view of man and his life is only to be found in the biblical perspective." He communicates penetrating issues in a warm, unthreatening manner.

In *The Meaning of Persons* Tournier tells about the challenge of his work. People see me, tell me stories about themselves, correct them in subsequent visits, all in order that I can understand them, he says. But each patient "remains an impenetrable mystery." How can we discover the true person? He quotes Pascal: "We strive continually to adorn and preserve our imaginary self, neglecting the true one." We are a mixture of opposites.

Tournier finds a powerful analogy in Adam and Eve after the fall, sewing fig leaves together to cover themselves. "But God himself soon came. . . . Instead of taking man's clothing away from him, God provides him with a finer garment." Then he cites the apostle Paul's injunction to put on the new man, born of the Spirit (Col. 3:9–10).

Central to Tournier's book is the distinction between the person (our true self) and the personage (what we reveal). We make efforts to isolate our person completely from our personage, but Tournier urges us to accept the "clothing" that God himself gives us—"the personage God wills us to have."

In another analogy, Tournier says each human being is like an orchestra with an internal conductor. "A margin of fluctuation is a characteristic of life," and the conductor motions to that instrument to tone down or speed up. In our lives, such fluctuations may bring us to a counselor's office, but fluctuations in themselves are healthy. They make our lives interesting.

Psychological counseling is a fairly new field, and Christians have climbed aboard only in the last few decades. Nowadays we see several different versions of Christian counseling and a slew of self-help books that address psychological issues. Paul Tournier is the father of them all, a pioneer in the field, an expert who brought his Christian faith into every aspect of his work.

Stride toward Freedom:
The Montgomery Story

1958

MARTIN LUTHER KING JR.

Martin Luther King Jr. was nervous. It was 1954 and this twenty-
five year old was preaching a trial sermon in his bid to become
pastor of the Dexter Avenue Baptist Church in Birmingham,
Alabama. The previous night he wrestled with uncertainty:
"Should I attempt to interest [the congregation] with a display
of scholarship? Or should I preach just as I had always done,
depending finally on the inspiration of the spirit of God? I
decided to follow the latter course. I said to myself over and over
again. 'Keep Martin Luther King in the background and God in
the foreground and everything will be all right. Remember you
are a channel of the gospel and not the source.'"

He got the job.

King could have taken a teaching job in the North, but
together he and his wife, Coretta, chose this pastorate in the
segregated South. "I'm not going to put my ultimate faith in the
little gods that can be destroyed in an atomic age," he preached
the following month, "but in the God who has been our help
in ages past, and our hope for years to come, and our shelter in
the time of storm, and our eternal home. That's the God that
I'm putting my ultimate faith in."

He was in his new church barely a month when Rosa Parks
was arrested for refusing to move to the back of a Birmingham
bus. Three days later he was surprised to be elected head of the
newly formed protest movement. At first he wasn't sure that a
boycott was a Christian action to take, but remembering Henry
Thoreau's comments on civil disobedience, he finally decided
that a boycott was simply saying, "We can no longer lend our
cooperation to an evil system."

At a mass meeting of the protesters, he urged, "We must keep God in the forefront. Let us be Christian in all of our actions. . . . It is not enough for us to talk about love. Love is one of the pivotal points of the Christian faith, [but] standing beside love is always justice and we are only using the tools of justice."

In his autobiography King comments, "It was the Sermon on the Mount. . . . It was Jesus of Nazareth that stirred the Negroes to protest with the creative weapon of love." Later King saw how to use "the Christian doctrine of love operating through the Gandhian method of nonviolence." The next month King was jailed for driving thirty miles an hour in a 25 mph zone. Threatening phone calls increased to twenty or thirty a day, and then his house was bombed.

Stride toward Freedom is mostly the story of the bus boycott, naturally autobiographical in part, and the rest an argument for nonviolence and racial change. King felt that leadership was thrust on him by God and he dare not refuse the mantle. Thus he became the voice and symbol of the nonviolent civil rights movement.

The events in Birmingham and the publication of *Stride toward Freedom* catapulted this young black pastor into the worldwide spotlight. The nation was a powder keg in those days, but King's commitment to nonviolence kept cooling the situation, even as his commitment to justice kept turning up the heat on the authorities. As this book makes clear, he wasn't making this up. It was the way of Jesus.

In the last chapter, "Where Do We Go from Here?" he calls on the church to change its racial policies. He found it appalling that "the most segregated hour of Christian America is eleven o'clock Sunday morning, the same hour when many are standing to sing, 'In Christ There Is No East or West.'"

King will always be remembered for his "I Have a Dream" speech delivered at the Lincoln Memorial. That's appropriate. While he did not shy away from pointing out the problems of society, he tempered his criticism with a vision of justice, the way life could be if we ran our civilization on godly principles. In 1968, when he was thirty-eight, King was assassinated in Memphis, Tennessee.

Basic Christianity

1958

JOHN STOTT

As a London schoolboy, John Stott attended a Christian Union meeting at which an evangelist nicknamed "Bash" Nash spoke on the subject, What shall I do with Jesus? Stott recalls, "That I needed to do anything with Jesus was an entirely novel idea to me." That night, however, he became a Christian.

He went on to study theology at Cambridge, and at twenty-four became curate of All Souls, Langham Place, in London (becoming rector there five years later). Located near London University, the BBC headquarters, and several major hospitals, the church under Stott's pulpit ministry drew many educated young adults. "God has given me an inquiring mind," Stott says, and that mind, coupled with his penchant for breaking with the standard evangelical thinking on some issues, has kept him popular with young audiences around the world. At the Lausanne World Congress in 1973 Stott stood with Christian leaders from Third World countries affirming the need to combine social concern with evangelism in our outreach to the world. He played a major role in giving Third World leaders a more prominent voice at future evangelical congresses.

"Above all else," he says, "we must preach Christ, and not Christ in a vacuum, but rather a contemporary Christ who once lived and died, and now lives to meet human need in all its forms."

During the 1950s Stott became well known for his speaking at universities throughout the United Kingdom and then in the United States. He was especially popular at the Urbana Missionary Conference, sponsored every three years by InterVarsity. His concern for young people compelled him to write *Basic Christianity*.

He writes: "Hostile to the church, friendly to Jesus Christ. These words describe large numbers of people, especially young people today. They are opposed to anything that savors of institutions."

And so Stott builds his structure from the ground up. His first chapter begins, "In the beginning, God." However, Stott is not assuming that his reader buys into a God-belief as yet. So he ends the chapter with a prayer that he asks the reader to pray: "God, if you exist (and I don't know if you do)," and so on.

Then his first main section is on Christ's Person. As he stated earlier, he had found most people to be "friendly to Jesus Christ," and so he builds on this. But then he proceeds into sections on man's need, Christ's work, and man's response. In that final section he discusses not only our duty to God but also our duty to the church and our duty to the world.

Though young adults are often turned off to the church, Stott is not. In fact he urges Christians not to neglect the church. In the book *Five Evangelical Leaders,* Christopher Catherwood calls Stott "a Calvary-centered radical. His book *Basic Christianity* makes this central fact clear—that it is through Christ on the cross we are saved. But equally, his works, such as *Christian Counter-Culture* on the Sermon on the Mount and *God's New Society* on Ephesians, demonstrate the life-changing consequences of a true conversion."

John Stott's balanced Christianity makes this book one that can be easily handed to non-Christians—and indeed it has been, with eternal effects.

The Gospel Blimp

1960

JOSEPH T. BAYLY

We have done some weird things in the name of evangelism.

In the 1960s we evangelicals were caught between our two natures. First, we were fundamentalists, holding to the basics of our Christian faith but also separating ourselves from the world. Since Billy Sunday's fiery rants, we had been warned against fraternizing with the enemy. "Mustn't drink, or smoke, or chew, or go around with those who do." So went our separatist nursery rhyme.

But in the 1940s and early '50s, our faith had been infused with a new energy. *Evangelicals* were fundamentalists with a new focus on the good news. We wanted to share it with as many people as possible. Youth organizations and mission agencies were spawned for that purpose. Church members were urged to evangelize their communities.

But we had a problem. How do you share your faith with people you're not supposed to "go around with"? We had been separated for so long, we had no clue who our neighbors were. How could we get the gospel across to them?

The tract.

It was just a slip of paper, folded over, with some gripping headline that would entice the recipient to open it up. "Don't go to Hell, for Heaven's sake!" or something like that. The inner pages would carry a message of salvation. The beauty of the tract was that you didn't actually have to talk with the object of your evangelism at all. You could avoid being tainted by their liquor breath or chewing tobacco, and still get the message across. Christian vacationers were advised to wrap tracts in cellophane and drop them among sunbathers at the beach. ("You Think It's Hot *Here?*")

Leave it to Joe Bayly to expose the silliness. Already a well-respected journalist and editor of InterVarsity's magazine, Bayly had a sharp wit and a keen eye for the foibles of the faithful. He wrote a regular column for *Eternity* magazine based on his random musings. It was called, "Out of My Mind."

In *The Gospel Blimp,* he applied his satire to our methods of evangelism. It was a fable, really, the simple story of a church that wanted to reach its community for Christ. The board considered its options and eventually came up with the perfect plan: Buy a blimp and drop tracts on the neighborhood. Never mind that they might actually be alienating those who had to rake the tracts from their back yards. Never mind that it might be far easier—and cheaper—simply to talk to their neighbors. No, the blimp plan was big and bold and—hey, what a witness! The delightful tale skewered our taste for spectacle, separation, committee meetings . . . and tracts.

With this and other writings, Bayly challenged Christians to be better, smarter, more biblical. He butchered a few sacred cows along the way. In one column, he talked about growing a beard and being criticized by one church woman. "What about the weaker brother?" she asked, brandishing a trump card that has long stifled Christian expression. "Weaker brother?" Bayly responded. "She seemed like a 'stronger sister' to me!"

Yet Bayly balanced his scathing wit with a sweet spirit. Readers knew they could count on him to make them laugh and to make them think. In a time when we evangelicals took ourselves very seriously, Bayly let some air out of our tires. With humor, he taught us humility.

The Psychology of Counseling

1960

CLYDE M. NARRAMORE

Some books are like doors; you open them and voilà!—you enter a new world. Other books are door openers. They open the passage so that others may go through.

Clyde M. Narramore, in *The Psychology of Counseling,* was a door opener. In the latter decades of the twentieth century, books by counselor/psychologists Dobson, Smalley, Harley, Chapman, Wright, and others made regular appearances on Christian best-seller lists. Who opened the door for them? {129}

By the year 2000, thousands of churches across America were employing psychological counselors, trained in marriage and family therapy. Who opened the door?

Today many evangelical seminaries are training pastors as well as psychological specialists in counseling for ministry in the churches of North America. Who opened the door?

The answer, of course, is Clyde Narramore. It's obvious that *The Psychology of Counseling* met a need, because it went through twenty printings within fifteen years of publication.

In the first half of the century, conservative Christians had lots of questions about psychology and psychiatry. To them it smacked of Freud and sex and pseudoscience. Yet pastors were finding that parishioners often came to them with problems they were not trained to answer. More and more of their time was spent in counseling and they were at a loss to know how to cope with the load.

With a doctorate from Columbia University and working as consulting psychologist on the staff of the Los Angeles County Superintendent of Schools, Narramore was a professional in the field. He had written some smaller books for Christian parents, such as *How to Tell Your Children about Sex* and *How to Understand and Influence Your Children.* His expertise was in the area of child psychology. But as pastors sought him out for help, he felt he had to do more. So he wrote *The Psychology of Counseling,* with the long subtitle *Professional Techniques for Pastors, Teachers, Youth Leaders and All Who Are Engaged in the Incomparable Art of Counseling.*

After an introductory section on how a minister should go about it ("Basic Concepts and Techniques of Counseling"), Narramore delves into specific areas of counseling with such chapters as "Counseling with Teenagers" (his specialty), "The Mentally and Emotionally Ill," "Basic Guides in Marriage Counseling," and "Problems of Sex." His final section, "The Use of Scripture in Counseling," is a valuable forty-page appendix.

Professionals criticized the book because of its too-pat answers to some complex problems and his heavy use of Scripture. Yet Narramore was not afraid to tackle subjects that might have daunted others—such as homosexuality.

Clyde Narramore was not the first Christian to write in this field. Wayne Oates and Seward Hiltner had written earlier for their specialized audiences, as had Ernest White in England with his excellent *Christian Life and the Unconscious,* but no one did as much in the area as Clyde Narramore.

He began a daily broadcast called *Psychology for Living,* which aired on nearly two hundred stations across the country; he started counseling centers in the East, Southwest, and West Coast; he launched *Psychology for Living* magazine; and then he founded a professional school, the Rosemead School, to train men and women for a ministry in counseling. Rosemead continues today as a branch of Biola University.

With all these efforts, Narramore brought psychological issues into Christian discussions. In a way, he gave evangelicals permission to consult modern psychology and psychiatry alongside the Bible for the answers to their problems. And he showed a way to integrate Christian belief with this professional field. Today we see the widespread results of Narramore's groundbreaking work.

Yes, it was quite a big door that Clyde Narramore opened.

The New Bible Dictionary

1961

J. D. DOUGLAS,
ORGANIZING EDITOR

Before this dictionary came along, most Christians had to depend on Bible dictionaries written in the 1800s. But after *The New Bible Dictionary* was published, and published successfully, {131} a score of others have appeared on the scene.

A one-volume Bible dictionary is almost a necessity for any involved lay Christian, whether he or she teaches a Sunday school class, attends a small-group Bible study, or just has lots of questions regarding the preacher's sermon. The most popular dictionary had been Smith's *Dictionary of the Bible,* which had been periodically updated but was still essentially a work from the 1880s. Sir William Smith had been an amazing scholar who taught Greek and Latin and became the outstanding lexicographer of the century. His reputation may have resulted from the fact that he had established a virtual monopoly on dictionaries, having written more than a half dozen of them from a *Dictionary of Greek and Roman Antiquities* to his *Dictionary of Christian Biography*. But his stellar achievement was his Bible dictionary.

Then in 1915 along came the *International Standard Bible Encyclopedia,* a monumental five-volume work, edited by James Orr. Soon ISBE, as it was known, became the sine qua non for most ministers. However, the price tag and the heft of the multiple volumes made it a stretch for most laypeople. *Hastings' Dictionary of the Bible,* in a one-volume format, was a noble effort, but it never supplanted Smith.

Finally in the 1950s, England's Inter-Varsity Fellowship felt the need to produce a one-volume Bible dictionary. Ronald Inchley, IVF's publications secretary, and J. D. Douglas were the key players, and from the start it was successful, both in Great Britain and in North America. J. D. Douglas, by the way, has gone on to serve as editor of almost as many dictionaries as Sir William did a century earlier. Among other works by Douglas are the *International Dictionary of the Christian Church* and *The New Twentieth-Century Encyclopedia of Religious Knowledge*. While Smith tended to be a bit stodgy, Douglas has a flair that often provides some unexpected discoveries for the reader.

After two decades of steady sales, the IVF dictionary was revised and updated by the Tyndale Fellowship for Biblical Research, an organization closely associated with IVF. Consulting editors on this update were F. F. Bruce of the University of Manchester, D. J. Wiseman of the University of London, J. I. Packer of Regent College in Vancouver, D. Guthrie of London Bible College, and A. R. Millard of the University of Liverpool. In addition, some two hundred contributors from both sides of the Atlantic as well as from Australia and New Zealand were involved in the new edition. Another difference in the new edition is that the Revised Standard Version of the Bible was used as the basic text instead of the King James.

Other Bible dictionaries came shortly after the 1962 publication. Merrill Tenney's *Pictorial Bible Dictionary*, published a year later, had the advantage of numerous illustrations, but it lacked the international flavor of biblical scholarship from around the world. *The Interpreter's Bible Dictionary*, a four-volume work, was an excellent companion volume to the *Interpreter's Bible Commentary*. It also appeared in 1962, but for the lay reader it had the disadvantage of being published in four pricey volumes, and for the evangelical its mixed bag of theology was a bit problematic.

Bible dictionaries generally begin with Aaron and end with Zuzim. They are not meant to be commentaries on the text, but rather to explain the meaning of Bible words and names. *The New Bible Dictionary* also explains biblical concepts. A section on education, for instance, gives background on the development of schools, teaching as a profession in Bible times, the scope of education, and methods and aims of education. It has an entry for the Dead Sea Scrolls, written by F. F. Bruce, and its entry on plants of the Bible was written by F. N. Hepper of the Herbarium at Kew's Royal Botanic Garden. Thus the dictionary provides authoritative entries about various Bible-related subjects as well as precise definitions of Bible names and places.

The Company of the Committed

1961

ELTON TRUEBLOOD

It may seem strange to hear a Quaker talk in military terms, but that's what Elton Trueblood does in this classic.

America was caught up in the excitement of exploring outer space. Trueblood, however, was more concerned about exploring inner space. "We have around us many new frontiers," he wrote, "but the most unexplored of all frontiers is that of a loving fellowship." Calling for "a task force of committed men and women who truly care for God, for the church, and for other people," Trueblood considered this book "a dynamic rallying point and a manual for action for every Christian."

Born and raised in a small town in Iowa, Trueblood began his education at a Quaker school in Oskaloosa, and went on to Brown University, Hartford Theological Seminary, and Harvard University, before getting his doctorate from Johns Hopkins in 1934. Strongly influenced by the writings of C. S. Lewis, he said at one point, "There's nobody in America doing what Lewis is doing in Britain. Why shouldn't I try?"

For nine years he served as chaplain at Stanford University, but it was while he was acting dean of chapel at Harvard that the idea for his first book came to him. *The Essence of Spiritual Religion* (1936) was based on the theme of "the abolition of the laity." As Trueblood saw it, everyone is called into ministry. "The word laity does not appear in the Bible," he emphasizes. "Christianity withers when it's a spectator sport. A layman in medicine is one who cannot practice. The same with law. But there is no place in the Christian faith for those who cannot or will not practice."

To encourage men and women to practice their ministry, he began the Yokefellow movement in 1952. At that time this was an unusual idea: small groups meeting each week to encourage one another in daily prayer, Bible reading, worship, and giving. But the concept soon spread throughout the world.

Trueblood wrote thirty-seven books before he died in 1995, but his most famous book is *The Company of the Committed*. We need to think of the Church in military terms, says this Quaker. But instead, we tend to think of it as a society with mild claims, a club that you can join whenever you wish, without any involvement. To counter this, the author suggests a five-point program:

1. *The necessity of commitment.* The church must win back its "lost provinces." What are these? They might differ from community to community, but he mentions the campus, young people, and labor as three provinces the church has by and large lost.

2. *A call to enlistment.* "The tide of secularism is rising," Trueblood noted (in 1961!), and it would take a strong army to stand against it. "The test of the vitality of a religion is to be seen in its effect upon culture."

3. *The vocation of witness.* A Christian must not be afraid to witness, and "all witness necessarily involves the use of the first person singular." That is, we must be willing to tell our personal stories of faith and transformation.

4. *A strategy of penetration.* The church building should become a drill hall equipping the soldiers to go out to do battle. "In church," he says, "we often spend our efforts promoting Sunday." But there are other days of the week when the battle is more intense for the soldiers. "The effective Christian pattern is always a base and a field. The base is the church; the field is the world." We need to strategize to see how best we can penetrate our areas of witness.

5. *The criterion of validity.* It is love in action that redeems society, Trueblood said, and that is what the world must see.

It was a time when the United States was nominally Christian but drifting away from Christian principles. Christians were isolating themselves in church activities that had little impact on the rest of their lives. Trueblood's rallying cry struck home with many Christians, who took the challenge to get serious about their faith and their mission.

The Genesis Flood

1961

JOHN C. WHITCOMB
and HENRY M. MORRIS

Creation science has been controversial within the evangelical community as well as in society at large, but there is no doubt of the impact of this book by Whitcomb and Morris, published by a small company, Presbyterian and Reformed Publishing, in 1961. By the end of the century the book had gone into its forty-first printing. {135}

Modern science holds that the earth is tremendously old. Its evidence: the layers upon layers of geologic rock formations that must have taken millions of years to lay down. This is called *uniformitarianism,* the belief that existing physical processes account for all past changes and consequently the present state of what we see now. Whitcomb and Morris feel that God's intervention in history (in particular Noah's universal flood) could account for the geological evidence.

Whitcomb and Morris do not deny uniformitarianism but they hold that God has intervened both at the time of the fall and at the time of the flood with supernatural catastrophic events. The record of earth history, they say, is "primarily a record of catastrophic intensities of natural processes, operating largely within uniform natural laws, rather than one of gradualism and relatively uniform process rates." Translation: A universal flood can explain things better than millions of years of gradual processes.

The concept is so controversial in the scientific community that even the writer of the book's foreword, the head of the geology department at the University of Southwestern Louisiana, had some professional reservations, finding these views "difficult to accept." Still, he encouraged Christians and non-Christians alike to consider seriously what Whitcomb and Morris were saying.

The 518-page volume looks first at the basic arguments for a universal flood and then at arguments against a universal flood.

Next, they consider ways that writers in the past have tried to harmonize a belief in the flood with scientific uniformitarianism. This is followed by ways that Christians can and should harmonize actual scientific evidence and Scripture. But the final two sections (more than half the book) deal with such subjects as the days of creation, the ice age, carbon 14 dating, buried forests, and so on.

The Whitcomb and Morris book came only seven years after Bernard Ramm's *The Christian View of Science and Scripture*. Whereas Ramm opened up the possibilities of a variety of positions that Christians might hold, Whitcomb and Morris felt that most of those positions were playing fast and loose with Scripture.

So John Whitcomb, who taught Old Testament at Grace Theological Seminary in Winona Lake, Indiana, and Henry Morris, with a Ph.D. from the University of Minnesota, teamed up to produce this work. Carefully written and well-documented, *The Genesis Flood* has since become a classic apologetic for biblical creationism and the universality of the flood described in Genesis.

The Whitcomb-Morris book wasn't the first book to challenge uniformitarianism—George McCready Price had done so in *Evolutionary Geology and the New Catastrophism* (1926)—but the timing was right and the evangelical public was ready for it. No matter how well Ramm and other evangelical scientists supported alternative positions, the average evangelical still suspected them of holding a lower view of the Bible. But there was no doubt about Whitcomb and Morris. They believed in the days of creation, the historicity of Adam and Eve, and the reality of a universal flood.

And so creation science became a major force. Henry Morris founded the Institute for Creation Research in 1970, first as a part of Christian Heritage College and later as a separate organization "devoted to research, publication, and teaching in those fields of science particularly relevant to the study of origins." The rise of the home school movement also abetted the creation science movement, and other books were published and organizations were launched, some very politically active. The creation science movement now has a substantial presence in the fields of science and education, all stemming from the influential book by Whitcomb and Morris.

Man: The Image of God

1962

G. C. BERKOUWER

Berkouwer's monumental achievement may have been the writing of his fourteen-volume *Studies in Dogmatics,* published between 1952 and 1976. But for many of us, it is a monumental achievement just to *read* fourteen volumes of theology.

Berkouwer stands as one of the most formidable theologians of the latter half of the century. He wasn't afraid to navigate his theological craft between the rocks of difficult straits, and that is also a monumental achievement.

While many of the other books in our elite list of one hundred from the past century will be forgotten, you can be sure that Berkouwer will not be. He stands tall as a theologian, and pastors and seminarians for the next several generations will be referring back to Berkouwer's *Studies in Dogmatics,* and maybe particularly to volume 8, *Man: The Image of God.*

You may wonder why it is necessary for contemporary theologians to even bother writing anymore. If Luther and Calvin wrote what they thought the Bible taught, why should we bother to tinker with that? Why don't we just parrot what's been said?

But a lot has gone on in the world in the last five hundred years. Especially when it comes to the study of humanity, the fields of psychology, philosophy, anthropology, and biology have all made some bold statements that nudge if not collide with historic Christian positions. And how do the writings of modern theologians like Barth, Brunner, and Bultmann affect the evangelical position?

What made Berkouwer particularly interesting is that he tended to be practical instead of abstract, and he enjoyed direct interaction instead of philosophical vagueness. Born in Amsterdam in 1903, he studied at the Free University at a time when Karl Barth's writings were starting to get attention. Not surprisingly, some of his first writings were attacks on Barthian theology. Before and during World War II, he was a pastor in the Netherlands and in 1945 he assumed the honored chair of dogmatics at the Free University. Having lived through the war, he was now concerned that theology relate to everyday existence. "The Word of God never desires to lead us to an empty systematic which does not touch concrete life."

While other theologians might begin their work with a book on the nature of God, Berkouwer begins with *Faith and Sanctification*. *Faith and Justification* is volume 3, *Faith and Perseverance*, volume 6. The road to faith, he says, is not reason, but simply the grace of God. He spells this out in *Man: The Image of God*. There he explains that sin has corrupted the whole of man. "There is no limit or boundary within human nature beyond which we can find some last human reserve untouched by sin; it is man himself who is totally corrupt." It is only by God's grace that we are saved.

This does not mean that man cannot think logically, but it affects the vital connection between the heart and the understanding. Since man is a combination of will, understanding, and emotions, sin is influential in every human decision.

Man: The Image of God is then the eighth volume in Berkouwer's theology set, following the three volumes on faith, *The Person of Christ, General Revelation, Divine Election,* and *The Providence of God.* Nearly half the book deals with questions regarding what it means for man to be in the image of God and whether we can still speak of man as being in that image. He opposes speculating on issues that Scripture does not deal with and he shies away from arguments regarding the nature and origin of the soul. "Nowhere in Scripture is the origin of the soul spoken of as a separate theme."

Sometimes you wish that Berkouwer would be more speculative and provide some nuggets of educated guesswork. But he sticks to Scripture, and that is what a biblical theologian is supposed to do.

A Wrinkle in Time

1962

MADELEINE L'ENGLE

"Artists of all disciplines must be willing to go into the dark, let go control, be surprised." So says author Madeleine L'Engle, describing something she has always done in her writing—especially in her children's books.

She made her big splash in 1962 with *A Wrinkle in Time,* a science fiction book that won the prestigious Newbery Award for children's fiction. That one book soon became four (her "Time Quartet" also includes *A Wind in the Door, A Swiftly Tilting Planet,* and *Many Waters*), with the same characters moving through time and space. Later books followed the same families, and later generations of those families, into new adventures. The loyal readers of *Wrinkle* lapped up each new volume. L'Engle has also published fiction for adults (notably *A Severed Wasp*), plays, poems, and books of essays and theological musings *(A Circle of Quiet).*

But her children's books remain her chief claim to fame. She has the touch, challenging young readers with some heady content, but maintaining a child's point of view. Meg, the preteen girl at the center of the "Time Quartet," is intelligent but self-doubting, sometimes loving, sometimes crabby—the kind of ordinary person most readers can identify with. She is thrown into otherworldly adventures with her precocious little brother (Charles Wallace) and her incipient boyfriend (Calvin). Along the way they all discover their world-saving powers—and they learn valuable lessons about good, evil, and love.

Reading *A Wrinkle in Time,* one thinks of C. S. Lewis's fiction—both his *Chronicles of Narnia* and his space trilogy *(Out of the Silent Planet, Perelandra, That Hideous Strength).* It's as if L'Engle took the best of both and then carried it all to a new level. As in the space trilogy, her characters hop through space to encounter primeval forces of good and evil. As in Narnia, her characters challenge the powers of evil with divine aid. But Lewis was always a theologian, using his fictional worlds to teach truth and explore his theories. L'Engle traffics in pure imagination.

As a result, these works are less overtly "Christian" than Lewis's. She's not retelling the Christ story in allegory, as Lewis did. She's telling new stories. If Lewis was Gospel, L'Engle is the book of Acts. She follows divinely guided people as they fight against fear, pride, and selfishness. You might say that she "teaches" the power of love and sacrifice, but there are no clear Christ-figures here. The lessons are not verbal but visual. We see Meg standing before the captive Charles Wallace. She says, "I love you. I love you."—using the only weapon she has against the evil that holds him. "I love you, Charles Wallace. I love you." And her brother comes out of his catatonic shell like Lazarus from the tomb.

Some of L'Engle's scientific imaginings are quite stunning, considering this was 1962 and she was writing for kids. She has a kind of "beaming" of molecules that predates *Star Trek* by several years. Her portrait of the town of Camazotz, in the grip of the evil It, is downright Orwellian in its eerie automation. And her explanations of time travel, dying stars, and the nature of light are cutting edge.

But the power of L'Engle's writing has always been in the deeply Christian nature of her imagination. Her nonfiction has made her Christian commitment explicit, but her fiction is deeply rooted in that commitment. Children and adults of all religions have tasted the love of God in the literary banquets she has served up. And as a Christian who writes for the world, she has inspired many other Christian writers and artists to break out of their pious constraints, to "be willing to go into the dark, let go control, be surprised."

Living Letters

1962

KENNETH N. TAYLOR

Most train commuters to Chicago bought a copy of the *Tribune* to read on the trip. Kenneth Taylor used the ride to paraphrase the Bible.

At home he and his wife, Margaret, had ten children, and { 141 } Taylor was concerned because his kids weren't understanding the family's devotional reading of the King James Version with its Elizabethan English. He began the project in 1954, finished the New Testament seven years later, and then began submitting it to various publishing houses. All rejected it, even though Taylor was employed by one of them and was well-known to all. But Taylor was convinced of the value of the product, so he and his wife decided to publish the New Testament epistles themselves in 1962. Their family savings were minimal, but they decided to invest all they had in the project.

At first the response was discouraging. *Living Letters* got little response at the Christian Booksellers Association in 1962. But early the following spring, Billy Graham bought a quantity and offered it on a telecast. Before Graham was finished with the offer, he had given away 500,000 copies. That was the start, but only the start. Taylor followed *Living Letters* with his "Living" paraphrases of the Gospels and Acts, then portions of the Old Testament, finally putting together *The Living Bible,* which was a phenomenal publishing success. Total sales now exceed forty million copies in the United States and Canada alone, and for two consecutive years in the 1970s it sold more copies than any book of any kind anywhere in the world.

The twentieth century was the century of excellent Bible translations and paraphrases, beginning with the American Standard Version in 1901. Selecting one hundred books that changed the century, we could have chosen several Bible translations. The Revised Standard Version, Phillips New Testament, New

American Bible, The New English Bible, Good News Bible, New International Version, New King James Version, and *The Message*—all these have made their mark on the century.

But in many ways *The Living Bible* was unique. It did not claim to be a word-for-word translation. It was a paraphrase, and it was targeting an evangelical market that believed in the infallibility of the very words of Scripture. The RSV had been roundly castigated for its renditions, and Taylor was venturing into the same arena. *The Living Bible* certainly received criticism as the work of a single paraphraser. Taylor admits in the preface to his first edition: "Whenever the author's exact words are not translated from the original languages, there is a possibility that the translator, however honest, may be giving the English reader something that the original writer did not mean to say. This is because a paraphrase is guided not only by the translator's skill in simplifying, but also by the clarity of his understanding of what the author meant and by his theology." But as a conservative himself, Taylor interpreted Scripture in keeping with his own theology, and that made his free, sometimes colloquial, paraphrase generally acceptable to the evangelical market.

Notable also is the fact that a large evangelical publishing company, Tyndale House, has blossomed out of the success of *The Living Bible*. In 1997 Tyndale House published the New Living Translation, a completely new work, which is not a paraphrase but a thought-for-thought translation by a team of ninety scholars. No doubt, it will make an impact on the twenty-first century.

Kenneth Taylor began his *Living Letters* by paraphrasing the first verse of Romans this way: "Dear Friends in Rome: This letter is from Paul, Jesus Christ's slave, chosen to be a missionary, and sent out to preach God's Good News." Little did he realize what would develop in the next couple of decades.

The Cross and the Switchblade

1963

DAVID WILKERSON
with JOHN *and* ELIZABETH SHERRILL

The flight of evangelical churches from the city to the suburbs was rampant during the first half of the twentieth century. Christians, cocooned in their havens, tried to forget about city prob- lems. Commuters were glad to be home, away from slum and smog, except for the newspapers tucked under their arms.

Gibson Winter's *The Suburban Captivity of the Churches* in the early 1960s was a telling indictment of all Protestant churches, but there were churches that bucked the trend, and individual Christians who felt the call of God to work in ghettos and slums and on skid rows.

One such individual was David Wilkerson, a young pastor from Phillipsburg, Pennsylvania. After reading a magazine story about the murder of a fifteen-year-old polio victim by a New York City gang called the Dragons, Wilkerson had the strange idea that God wanted him to go "to New York City and help those boys." The idea seemed ridiculous.

"Me? Go to New York? A country preacher barge into a situation he knows less than nothing about?"

Soon Wilkerson and his wife, Gwen, were driving across the George Washington Bridge into the heart of Harlem and Brooklyn. There was something captivating about this young man, naive as he was, who braved the gangs of the city, believing that if God wanted him to work in the city, God would protect him.

Once he confronted two gang leaders and told them they needed to give their lives to Jesus Christ. "And before my astonished eyes, these two leaders of one of the most feared fighting gangs in all of New York slowly dropped to their knees. Their War Lords followed their lead. They took their hats off and held them respectfully in front of them. Two of the boys had been smoking. Each took his cigarette out of his mouth and flipped it away, where it lay smoldering in the gutter while I said a very short prayer.

"'Lord Jesus,' I said, 'here are four of your own children, doing something that is very, very hard. They are kneeling here before everyone and asking you to come into their hearts and make them new. They want you to take away the hate and the fighting and the loneliness. They want to know for the first time in their lives that they are really loved. They are asking this of you, Lord, and you will not disappoint them. Amen.'"

When Wilkerson went home and recounted the story to his wife, he said he could hardly believe what had happened. She responded, "David, don't you realize that you got exactly what you wanted? . . . People who don't believe in miracles shouldn't pray for them."

His dramatic confrontations with gangs and the amazing conversions that followed enthralled Christians and non-Christians alike. In ten years eleven million copies of the book were in print and a major movie, starring Pat Boone and Erik Estrada, was released in theaters across the country. In addition, the Teen Challenge ministry Wilkerson founded was expanding into many major cities throughout the United States and the world.

Through his book, David Wilkerson not only alerted Christians to the desperate needs of the inner city but also showed them that something could be done about inner-city problems. The problems were certainly overwhelming, but God was raising up men and women to work with the troubled youths in the inner cities of America, and *The Cross and the Switchblade* had a lot to do with it.

The Broadway musical *West Side Story,* depicting life in New York City's gangs, had opened at the Winter Garden Theatre in 1957 and ran for 732 performances before going on tour. The film version starring Natalie Wood was released in 1961. But *West Side Story* was fiction, a musical version of Shakespeare's *Romeo and Juliet. The Cross and the Switchblade* was current news and it demonstrated that God had not given up on the city, and there was no reason for Christians to do so either.

They Speak with Other Tongues

1964

JOHN SHERRILL

You might say that the twentieth century was the century of the charismatic. As historian Mark Noll says in *Turning Points: Decisive Moments in the History of Christianity,* "In 1900 there were, at most, a bare handful of Christians who were experiencing special gifts of the Holy Spirit similar to those recorded in the New Testament. By the end of the century, as many as 500 million (or more than a quarter of the worldwide population of affiliated Christian adherents) could be identified as Pentecostal or charismatic."

Modern-day Pentecostalism can be traced back to a revival in 1906 at a small mission on Azusa Street in Los Angeles. The distinctive characteristic of Pentecostals is the belief that the "baptism in the Holy Spirit" is evidenced by speaking in tongues.

For the first half of the century, the movement flourished, thanks to the vigor of the Assemblies of God and other Pentecostal denominations. Evangelists like Oral Roberts and groups like the Full Gospel Business Men's Fellowship spread the movement beyond the denominations.

But it wasn't until April 3, 1960—when Dennis Bennett of the St. Mark's Episcopal Church in Van Nuys, California, announced to his congregation that he had received the gift of speaking in tongues—that the charismatic movement (or neo-Pentecostalism) was launched. *Time* and *Newsweek* carried Bennett's story, giving the movement national publicity. Bennett wrote of his experience in the book *Nine O'clock in the Morning,* which we could have easily included on our list.

Instead we include John Sherrill's *They Speak with Other Tongues,* published in 1964. Like Bennett, Sherrill was an Episcopalian, but a layman, and a more or less nominal one at that. Through a cancer scare and the witness of Catherine Marshall

LeSourd, he made his "leap of faith" and established a personal connection with Jesus Christ.

But a year afterward, as the "high" of his conversion experience was beginning to level off, he started hearing of the Pentecostal experience and began to investigate it. *They Speak with Other Tongues* tells Sherrill's story, first of his own conversion, and then of his investigation. He talks about the history of the movement and then his conversations and correspondence with numerous people who were identified with it. The book reads with journalistic style as well as a feeling of investigative reporting. He tells both sides, what he likes and what he is suspicious of. And in the end, in 1960, the same year that Bennett had his experience, Sherrill spoke in tongues.

Sherrill continued to use his writing talent to aid the Christian community. In subsequent years Sherrill with his wife, Elizabeth, wrote or cowrote numerous best-sellers, including *The Cross and the Switchblade, The Hiding Place,* and *God's Smuggler.*

But how did *They Speak with Other Tongues* change the century? For one thing, it sold about a million copies in the United States, besides its translations into other languages. The charismatic movement had now crossed over into the mainline Protestant denominations. But more specifically, it was after students and faculty at Duquesne University read this book in 1967 that a charismatic renewal broke out in the Roman Catholic Church. Later the Pope paved the way for greater acceptance of the movement by decreeing the charismatic gifts to be useful and necessary to the church. Today members of the Roman Catholic Church make up a significant part of the charismatic movement worldwide.

Spiritual Depression

1965

MARTYN LLOYD-JONES

When you consider all of the author's great expositions of Scripture, it may seem strange that we've selected a book that isn't. But although Lloyd-Jones is best known as a preacher, he had been trained as a physician and had practiced medicine before he went into the ministry. Though he wrote dozens of books on verse-by-verse Bible study and Reformed theology, his most widely acclaimed book is *Spiritual Depression: Its Causes and Cure.*

{ 147 }

As Christopher Catherwood wrote in his biographical sketch of Lloyd-Jones (*Five Evangelical Leaders,* Harold Shaw Press, 1985), *Spiritual Depression* is a key to understanding the man. It not only demonstrates his spiritual insight but also reveals two other important sides of his life. "He was very much the pastor as well as the preacher, and . . . he was greatly helped in his pastoral work by his medical training."

"You cannot isolate the spiritual from the physical," he wrote, "for we are body, soul, and spirit." Even something like over-tiredness has spiritual effects, he noted. Yet the ultimate causes of spiritual depression were the devil and human unbelief. Many Christians struggle with depression because they aren't sure of their salvation; sometimes they don't fully rest in the truth of justification by faith.

Sometimes depression comes from the idea that once a person is converted, life will be happy ever after. But Christians should have a better understanding of Satan's wiles than that. Lloyd-Jones speaks of the "balance of the Christian life, which is found in obedience (the will), coming from the heart (the emotions), guided by sound doctrine (the mind)."

The New Testament confirms that Christians are always facing trials and temptations, Lloyd-Jones points out. Paul speaks of the "fight of faith," but within each Christian is the Holy Spirit, who is called the Spirit of power and the Spirit of love.

The Christian is also reminded of God's forgiveness through the death of Christ. "Christianity," says Lloyd-Jones, "is common sense." If you are dominated by your feelings, you get into trouble, but the "great antidote to spiritual depression," he says, is understanding biblical doctrine.

Born in Wales, Martyn Lloyd-Jones entered medical school in London when he was only sixteen years old, and there he studied under Sir Thomas Horder, the royal physician, who was the leading physician of his day. He never forgot the value of asking questions before making a diagnosis, a practice that greatly helped him in the Christian ministry. Though he never had any formal theological training, he made the switch from medicine to a pulpit ministry after only a few years in medical practice. He became the minister of the Bethlehem Forward Movement Mission Church in Aberavon, Wales, with a working-class congregation. Within a few years he was hailed as the greatest Welsh preacher since the Welsh revival of 1904. Then in 1939 he accepted a call to become pastor of Westminster Chapel in London, succeeding G. Campbell Morgan. He stayed there for the next thirty years.

"He became probably the most influential evangelical leader in Britain," says Oliver Barclay of the British Inter-Varsity, and this was partly because he helped evangelicals gain a new confidence in biblical truth and historic Christian doctrine.

The Kingdom of the Cults

1965

WALTER R. MARTIN

The outstanding work on cults in the twentieth century has been Walter R. Martin's *The Kingdom of the Cults*. It was preceded by J. R. Van Baalen's *The Chaos of Cults*, John Gerstner's *The Theology of the Major Sects,* and earlier by G. Atkins's *Modern Religious Cults and Movements,* but Martin's 443-page, 15-cult analysis clearly replaced them.

{ 149 }

In the final decades of the century, cults have generally been defined as groups that are dangerous socially and led by a charismatic leader, luring impressionable youths into psychological bondage. But Martin identifies a cult (as does Charles Braden in *These Also Believe*) as "any religious group which differs significantly, in some one or more respects as to belief or practice, from those religious groups which are regarded as the normative expressions of religion in our total culture." In other words, by identifying a group as a cult, Martin is not charging it with being malicious, criminal, and damaging to the psyche. Certainly the Unitarians, which are included in his mix, have had many people who have made great contributions to society. But they are included because Unitarian beliefs are divergent from Christian beliefs in major areas.

The book also has chapters on Jehovah's Witnesses, Christian Science, Mormonism, Spiritism, Father Divine, Theosophical Society, Zen Buddhism, Swedenborgianism, Bahai, Black Muslims, Unity, Anglo-Israelitism, and Rosicrucianism. His most lengthy treatment, however, deals with Seventh-day Adventism, which after thorough investigation, he concluded was not a cult after all. Though it had some cultlike appearances: a strong leader, writings that supplement Scripture, and some unique beliefs, its core beliefs were in accord with historic Christianity.

Quoting from the writings of each group, Martin looks to see how each cult considers key Christian doctrines, such as Scripture, the Trinity, Jesus Christ, salvation and atonement, and the resurrection. Most chapters begin with a review of the cult's history, then explore the group's theological structure.

In early chapters, "Scaling the Language Barrier" and "The Psychological Structure of Cultism," Martin points out how cults redefine historic doctrines in ways that can easily make the average Christian think there is no difference at all. "Let it never be forgotten," he warns, "that cultists are experts at lifting texts out of their respective contexts, without proper concern for the laws of language, or the established principles of biblical interpretation."

The Kingdom of the Cults has thus become a valuable reference book for use when cultists come knocking at the door—not to mention when a family member gets involved in one. Some of the older cults seem to have their belief systems stabilized, but others are still in flux. The Worldwide Church of God founded by Herbert W. Armstrong, for instance, is a far different group now than it was when Martin wrote about it. Some of the newer cults, particularly those with Eastern roots, have been imported to America since Martin's classic book was published.

Because the average cult today is much more aggressively evangelistic than the average Christian church, the problem of cults is increasing. As long as cults continue to meet psychological and social needs that churches are not meeting, books like Martin's will be important resources for evangelical Christians.

The Taste of New Wine

1965

KEITH MILLER

"Taste and see that the LORD is good," the psalmist wrote (34:8). That's pretty much the thesis of Keith Miller's refreshing book. His title is an apt metaphor. You might say the church of the mid-1960s was manufacturing the wine, bottling the wine, marketing the wine—but few were actually *tasting* it. Miller exclaims that the Christian life must be more than a matter of holding correct doctrines. We must experience a relationship with Jesus Christ!

{ 151 }

This idea of Christianity as a relationship rather than a religion may seem hackneyed to you now. But in 1965 it was revolutionary. Miller, who was directing a spiritual-growth conference center in Texas at the time, was calling Christians to live what they said they believed. He mentioned in the preface to this book that when he invited conference participants to write anonymous questions, "they secretly tell us that they do not know how to pray, how to witness to other people about Christ without being embarrassed, how to simply communicate with their wives and families, or how to approach their vocational and social lives as committed Christians." It's interesting that these questions had to be anonymous. Christians were *supposed* to know all these things, and few would openly admit that they didn't.

So Miller's first challenge is "a new honesty." It was a time of pretense, both inside and outside the church. People were taught to pretend everything was okay when it wasn't. This had to change, Miller said. "We must realize that our fellowship is incurably crippled until and unless we recognize and face squarely the nature and extent of our deceitfulness with God, with each other, and with ourselves."

Miller modeled his new honesty in the pages of his book, illustrating many of his points with stories from his own life, from his marriage, and from his business. This too seems old hat to us today. We're used to public confessionals and tell-all memoirs.

But Miller was doing something new, especially for the church. He was admitting that he struggled, that he didn't have all the answers, that he was learning new things as he went along.

The book goes on to talk about commitment, family life, prayer, support groups, and living for Christ in the business world. Miller himself was a businessman with an oil company before he came to the conference center, so he spoke from experience. As he challenged people to let their faith infect their daily lives on the job, he knew it wasn't easy. This short chapter touches on issues that Christians in business are still exploring today. Miller challenged his readers to try to see their vocation as a *Christian* calling, but he also noted, ". . . Christ does not promise the businessman great material success in his vocation . . . but rather Christ brings the *inner security* which one seeks through great material success . . . and having found this, the burden of succeeding is lifted."

Miller was also ahead of his time in his chapter on sharing the new wine. He charged that Christians had "cheapened" the Christian message, that we should never see people as "prospects" for the church or "objects" for our witness. Instead, we should try to "listen to people with the idea in mind of making friends for Christ." Miller recommends that we respect people's privacy and not be too anxious to try to convince them. We should merely be honest about the role of Jesus in our lives, and encourage them to be honest with God as well.

Honesty is the best policy. It was sadly lacking in the church of Miller's day, but this book helped people begin to be more open about themselves. We should note another book that almost made our list, *Honest to God* by John A. T. Robinson (1963). That book also challenged the church, as Robinson opened up about modern struggles with traditional theology. *Honest to God* had significant impact on the mainline denominations, but from an evangelical perspective, Robinson was questioning too much. His honesty seemed to lead to a greater alienation from God. On the contrary, Miller's book hit home with evangelicals, because he was asking questions that led to a closer relationship with Christ.

Know Why You Believe

1967

PAUL E. LITTLE

"What is faith?" asked the Sunday school teacher.

A young boy answered in a flash, "Believing something you know isn't true."

That's how Paul Little began his classic apology for the faith, *Know Why You Believe.* Little was serving as director of evangelism for InterVarsity Christian Fellowship and had already penned the helpful *How to Give Away Your Faith.* Later he would add another volume: *Know What You Believe,* presenting basics of Christian belief. It's an impressive trilogy that squarely meets its audience—young people considering Christianity, accepting it, and wanting to share it with their friends.

Of course faith is *not* "believing something you know isn't true." Christian faith works side by side with intellectual exploration. Becoming a Christian, Little says, "does not mean kissing your brains good-bye."

But that wasn't always the accepted wisdom. For the first half of the twentieth century, fundamentalist Christianity had a decidedly anti-intellectual bias. After all, colleges were teaching Darwin, Marx, and Freud and questioning Christian dogma. Kids would leave the farm, go to college, and lose their faith. The church had no answers for the skeptics. One main reason for the anemia of the fundamentalist churches in the 1930s was that they *had* kissed their brains good-bye.

The evangelical movement of the 1940s and '50s brought a new attention to evangelism but it also recovered an interest in scholarship. Among the many new organizations founded in that period were new Christian colleges and seminaries, as well as ministries to young people in high school and college. InterVarsity Christian Fellowship sprang up in the 1930s and 1940s to help Christian kids keep their beliefs during college years. This would happen through the support of a Christian fellowship but also through instruction in the intellectual basis for Christianity.

And that's the job that Little takes on in *Know Why You Believe*. With only 108 pages, it's not a catalog of Christian truth (like the later *Evidence That Demands a Verdict* by Josh McDowell), but its brevity is a plus. This is no college text to pile on top of other assignments, just a book a student can tuck in his back pocket and skim in an hour or so at the dining hall.

It doesn't answer every question, but it covers the big ones: Is there a God? Is Jesus Christ God? Did Christ rise from the dead? Are the Bible documents reliable? Are miracles possible? and several others. There is something of C. S. Lewis in the tone of this book. It draws the reader into its own world of evidence and logic, coolly explaining why Christianity is reasonable. Little's avuncular style inspires confidence and affection. He's not shouting down the skeptics but embracing them. This is consistent with InterVarsity's style. Evangelism is never just proving a point but establishing a relationship.

Little's books have all proven to be valuable resources for students and Christian workers. They have strongly influenced at least one generation, not only with their solid content but also with their Christian character.

Christy

1967

CATHERINE MARSHALL

Like most writers, Catherine Marshall wanted to write a novel sometime in her life. Her first two books, *Mr. Jones, Meet the Master* (1950) and *A Man Called Peter* (1951), both nonfiction, had given her a name in the publishing world. In *To Live Again* (1957), she told of her struggle with grief and how "out of the heart's need," it is possible to creep humbly back "to acknowledge that need and to rejoin the human race." Once again she was acclaimed for her nonfiction writing. But she had a dream to write fiction.

And she knew what the novel would be about. Her mother had told her enough about her early days teaching school in the Smoky Mountains. The stories she told were so graphic and heartwarming, Catherine wanted to preserve them. So the aspiring novelist made two trips with her mother back into the Smokies, so Catherine could see, feel, smell, and hear what it was like.

In 1959 she remarried (her first husband, noted pastor Peter Marshall, the subject of *A Man Called Peter,* had died in 1949). Her new husband was Leonard LeSourd, editor of *Guideposts* magazine. A methodical man, he kept a notebook for prayer requests and answers. After his marriage to Catherine, one of the first prayer requests in his little notebook was, "That household help be found so that Catherine can continue the writing of her novel *Christy.*"

The help was soon found, but it took eight more years of research, writing, and rewriting before Catherine could complete *Christy.* It was published in 1967, and the public loved it. A quarter million hardbacks and four million paperbacks were sold. The *Dallas Times Herald* called it "an epic novel." The *St. Louis Post-Dispatch* said it was "a novel of celebration . . . wholesome, enjoyable, inspiring." The *Richmond Times-Dispatch* said it was "a good deal more than an inspiring story—it is a first-rate novel written in a style that is both skillful and gripping, a novel to be read more than once with undiminished enjoyment."

Catherine dedicated the novel to her mother, Leonora, whose story it was. (Catherine said it was 65 percent true.) On one visit back to the mountains, Leonora had told her daughter, "I'm not the one to put it on paper. You know, sometimes the dreams of the parents must be fulfilled in the children." And as Catherine said later, "Suddenly I understood how the story should be written—through mother's eyes."

So the story follows nineteen-year-old Christy Huddleston, who leaves her Asheville, North Carolina, home one Sunday morning in 1912 and boards a train bound for Cutter Gap in the Smokies. There she would teach school and come to know and love the mountain people. There her own faith would be tested and her heart would be torn.

Nearly a generation after the book was published, it was made into a CBS series, starring Kellie Martin, Tess Harper, and Tyne Daly. Then new children's books were written using the same basic characters and setting. But in between the initial publication and the TV reproduction, the success of the book was opening the eyes of media moguls to the potential of good, heartwarming family stories in the simpler life of the early 1900s.

If *Christy* had been so successful in touching America's heart, why not try other kinds of similar stories? So the Walton family became part of America's TV fare during the 1970s and 1980s. After that came the popular *Little House on the Prairie,* adapted from the books by Laura Ingalls Wilder.

In a day when family values were being jettisoned and traditional morality was being left behind, American families seemed to be telling TV networks that there was still a market for shows that would strengthen the home and build character in children.

Move Ahead
with Possibility Thinking

1967

ROBERT H. SCHULLER

It wasn't his best book nor his most substantive nor his best- seller, of which he has had several that made the national lists, but it was one of his first and it characterizes his very effective and amazing ministry. Robert Schuller has put a "happy face" on Christianity, which for much of the century was character- ized by a sad one. He has led the Christian church, as well as individual Christians, into becoming possibility thinkers, instead of being stymied by impossibilities.

In 1955, at the age of twenty-nine, Robert Schuller left a grow- ing church in Chicago, which he had seen swell from thirty- eight to about five hundred in five years. With his wife, Arvella, and five hundred dollars in assets, he headed west, landing in Orange County, south of Los Angeles. He rented the Orange Drive-in Theater and conducted Sunday services from the roof of the snack bar, while Arvella played the organ.

That drive-in theater and the title of this book have charac- terized his approach. It might be called a combination of Nor- man Vincent Peale (for positive thinking), Donald McGavran (for church growth), and Billy Graham (for evangelism). His approach has always been to keep the front door open as wide as possible to make it as easy as possible for visitors to enter. The drive-in theater in southern California fit well with his dreams.

By restructuring the church to meet the needs of southern California, he soon built a megacongregation, started an inter- national TV outreach *(The Hour of Power),* and began writing books. His massive twenty-million-dollar Crystal Cathedral in Garden Grove now is the home for a ten thousand–member congregation.

Critics charge him with accommodating Christianity to a narcissistic culture. He says he is merely repackaging his Reformed theology to reach the masses. There is no denying that his "possibility thinking" approach is a variant of the "positive thinking" philosophy of his mentor, Norman Vincent Peale. Schuller emphasizes the positive, not the negative. "People know they are sinners," he has said. "You don't need to remind them all the time. They are laden with guilt." In his book *Self-Esteem: A New Reformation,* he says that the basis of sin is a lack of self-esteem.

Move Ahead with Possibility Thinking is typical of his practical approach. In it he says we must remove the "impossibility complex" and he lists eight steps to do it, including the use of "prayer power." Next he shows the reader six ways to spot opportunities. If your woes are financial, he gives ten ways to overcome money problems; if the problems deal with wasting time, he provides ten tips of time management. Then there are ten steps to regenerate your energy supply, and finally he takes the reader into eight steps of mountain-moving faith, the last of which is "accepting" or surrendering. He writes, "We all face situations when our mountain does not budge. Then we pray with Jesus, 'Thy will be done.'"

At that point he introduces the reader to Jesus, "the greatest possibility thinker who ever lived." He closes with "five steps to help you find constructive possibilities in a personal heartbreaking experience." His approach is intensely practical. He opens the door wide at the beginning, and then he presents Jesus as the answer toward the end.

With a strategy like this, Schuller has created an extremely successful church and written thirty books. He has also founded the Institute for Successful Church Leadership, which has helped pastors from around the world find ways of inspiring their churches, not only in numerical growth but also in spiritual revival. His goal is to bring as many people as possible into the church; once they are there, the Christian education program of the church and its small-group ministry can nurture them into the Christian faith.

Schuller himself is the best twentieth-century example of a man who has moved ahead with possibility thinking.

The God Who Is There

1968

FRANCIS SCHAEFFER

They were failures. Francis and Edith Schaeffer, American missionaries in Switzerland, didn't know what to do. Within a few months, their son contracted polio, their mission board urged churches to stop supporting them, an avalanche almost wiped them out, and the Swiss government ordered them to leave the country. Friends were suggesting that Francis pastor a church back in the States or teach in a seminary.

But Francis Schaeffer felt that God was leading him to start something new, an *abri* (the French word for *shelter*). After an amazing turn of events in which the Swiss government annulled the edict against them, the Schaeffers established a home in Switzerland as a "spiritual shelter" for whoever wanted help. Surprisingly, news spread that somewhere buried deep in the Alps was a place where college and university students could get honest answers to life's deepest questions. And when the students went on their way, they told others of remarkable conversions, both spiritually and mentally.

What was remarkable about Francis Schaeffer was his broad sweep of knowledge. Critics complained about his generalizations, but students were amazed to see how he made everything fit together—from music to the fine arts, to philosophy, to psychology, to religion. In their university classrooms, their professors were specialists in targeted areas. Schaeffer was a generalist, who put the pieces together in a rational way.

Although he had written books for children, Schaeffer's first major book was *Escape from Reason* (1968), which was edited from tape recordings of his talks at conferences in England and Holland. In the book, Schaeffer analyzed the trends in modern thought, going back into the Middle Ages with Thomas Aquinas and Leonardo da Vinci, and including the more recent philosophies of Georg Hegel and Søren Kierkegaard. He showed how the floodgates of rationalistic knowledge were opened up by building on the intellectual tradition of Greece and Rome instead of on biblical revelation.

The God Who Is There, which is the first book deliberately written by Schaeffer instead of being transcripts of his lectures, begins where *Escape from Reason* leaves off. He found that not only students in secular universities but also students in Christian colleges needed what he had to offer. *The God Who Is There* charges that philosophers are dismissing as irrational everything that gives meaning to our lives. Modern theology has played along with that idea by promoting relativism and a mysterious leap of faith. Schaeffer also blamed neoorthodox scholars for using orthodox terminology, but denoting something far different from what Christianity has traditionally meant. Then he showed how the historic Christian faith has an integrity of its own.

Schaeffer is one of a number of thinkers in the century who fought for the intellectual integrity of the Christian faith. Some evangelicals who had abandoned the faith when they bumped up against secular professors in their universities reclaimed Christianity through reading Schaeffer's books.

The trilogy of Schaeffer books giving the core of his thinking (he wrote more than twenty books and booklets) concludes with *He Is There and He Is Not Silent,* which talks about how we can know God. In previous books he demonstrated the lack of answers of philosophies outside of biblical Christianity, but in this book he shows where the answers are. Apart from God's existence and his communication to us through Scripture and his Son Jesus Christ, he says, we will never find answers to the fundamental human questions.

Schaeffer had his critics, but he had an unforgettable way of bringing truth together. Specialists in philosophy or the arts could pan his generalistic thinking, but Schaeffer thought of himself primarily as an evangelist winning students to Christ and he certainly did that. He was also, of course, an apologist stating the claims of Christian faith in a way that made sense to students. And many evangelicals appreciate him as a man who started them thinking about Christ not only as Savior but as Lord of all, including nature, culture, science, and philosophy.

Dare to Discipline

1970

JAMES DOBSON

In 1970 James Dobson was a thirty-four-year-old school psychologist in southern California, unknown to the rest of the
world. He had his Ph.D. and had been named associate clinical
professor of pediatrics at the University of Southern California
School of Medicine.

{ 161 }

But then his first book, *Dare to Discipline,* came out and that
changed everything. The public response was so favorable that
he developed a series of workshops on the subject and then a
video series based on those workshops. The video series spawned
the *Focus on the Family* radio program, and in 1977 Dobson
founded the organization called Focus on the Family.

Dare to Discipline has sold more than three million copies,
Dobson's *Hide or Seek* has sold over a million, and he has written a dozen other books, each one of which broke into the best-
seller ranks on publication. His first film series, *Focus on the Family,* has been seen by more than seventy million people. The
next film series, *Turn Your Heart toward Home,* was released in
1986 and continues its international circulation. A third series,
Life on the Edge, released in 1984, was designed to help late teens
bridge the gap between adolescence and young adulthood. His
radio programs are heard on more than 2,900 radio facilities in
North America and in seven languages on approximately 1,300
facilities in more than seventy other countries.

Besides Dobson's own works, the Focus organization and
radio show often throw their weight behind other books as well.
If an author gets an on-air interview with Dobson, that's as sure
a mark of success in the Christian world as a guest spot on *Oprah*
is in secular publishing. Focus has clout. Today the organization, located now in Colorado Springs, ranks as one of the largest
parachurch organizations in the world.

And it all started in 1970 with a book. The title, *Dare to Discipline,* has led to some willful misunderstanding among Dobson's critics. Some say he advocates child beating, and that is certainly not the case. The book merely says that children need love, trust, affection . . . and discipline. Parents face the enduring challenge of helping children grow into responsible adults, and that means maintaining order and developing responsibility in children. Dobson maintains that discipline is part of the package and cannot be neglected by responsible parents.

Dobson's book hit the scene just as the influence of permissive-parenting experts was cresting. Parents had been told to withhold discipline, to let kids choose for themselves. *Dare to Discipline* found an audience with parents whose homes were in chaos, parents who sensed that there must be a better way. On the subject of discipline, Dobson was a lonely voice in the wilderness for about a decade, but then others started echoing his cries. Even now, when so many parents seem to be neglecting their children and when there are so many conflicting influences on children from media, school, and peers, Dobson's message finds a ready market.

Because of his fame in the evangelical community and because of his political views, he was appointed to several different commissions and study groups during the Reagan White House years. Those who don't share his political views may criticize the mixing of politics with his Focus on the Family ministry, but he believes that public policy, as well as the moral climate set in Washington, certainly has a strong effect on the families of the nation.

Whether you agree with James Dobson or not, you cannot disagree that the publication of his book in 1970 had tremendous implications on the evangelical scene for the last thirty years of the century.

The Meaning of the City

1970

JACQUES ELLUL

Some consider Jacques Ellul a prophet. Some consider him dangerous. Some think him a Bible-thumping technophobe. Some can't understand him.

This French scholar, who taught for more than a third of the century at the University of Bordeaux, has always been his own man. During World War II, he was dismissed from the university for protesting the Nazi occupation, and he joined the French Resistance, helping Jews escape. Maybe that experience implanted in him one of his main themes: the inherent evils of the modern world. The Nazis were certainly trying to build a "brave new world" but scuttled basic morality and human worth. Throughout his writings, Ellul has warned of the evil impulses that lie behind modern "advances."

Ellul, who died in 1994, was a respected social commentator and Bible scholar, yet he had no shortage of critics. Conservatives didn't trust him because of his Marxist and universalist tendencies. But liberal scholars were troubled by his devotion to the Bible as a complete document, God's Word to humanity, rather than a hodgepodge of culturally based myths. Like Karl Barth (one of Ellul's major influences), he was too biblical for some, but not fundamentalist enough for others.

But he certainly did his homework. His social commentaries offer penetrating insight and his biblical exposition is thorough. He saw every connection there was to see, weaving everything together in a persuasive argument. Pessimistic, but persuasive.

There are forces around us, he says, forces that do not help us or bring us closer to God—technology, money, the drive that compels us to gather in cities. These are basic elements of the human experience, but . . . well, that's the point. Humans are fallen creatures. We can't expect our human pursuits to win us salvation, but many of us do.

The Meaning of the City is an exquisite study of virtually everything the Bible says and implies about "the city." (Ellul often wrote theological companions to his social books. This is the follow-up to *The Technological Society*.) He has a lot to draw from. The city appears from Genesis—Genesis 4, to be precise, where Cain tries to get a new start by building a city—to Revelation. Ellul sees this as a rebellious act, as Cain refuses to wander the earth. From the start, then, the city is a human endeavor that sort of thumbs its nose at God. We see this again at Babel. Ellul tenaciously traces this theme throughout Scripture: Cities tend to oppose God, with a few exceptions . . . like Jerusalem, a "holy city" chosen by God as an example and witness to the nations. And, oddly, it was this city's opposition to Jesus that provided the way of redemption to the world, as Jerusalem's citizens crucified Jesus outside their city.

Thus the history of the world is written in its cities. Ellul makes it clear that he's not doing public relations for the country by badmouthing the city. It's just that "civilization is expressed by a city," he says. People create cities and instantly those cities become parasites, drawing all outside activities in. Whatever is wrong with humanity is wrong with the city, and it's taken to the nth power.

And yet, Ellul notes, the last chapter of God's drama is a new city, the heavenly Jerusalem coming to earth. It's as if God is saying, "You want a city? I'll give you a city! But it's my kind of city." So he redeems even this long-lasting symbol of rebellion.

Ellul's ideas are proving prophetic, as the new millennium anticipates continuing growth in megacities worldwide. While there are many Christians who "work for the welfare of the city," there are also numerous moral problems inherent in an urban setting. Ellul was also a lonely voice against the rise of technology, the manipulative power we give our machines. In our computer age, we need to heed his cautions.

The Late Great Planet Earth

1970

HAL LINDSEY
with CAROLE C. CARLSON

Armageddon, 1988. Well, Hal Lindsey didn't say that exactly but that was the implication. Hal Lindsey's runaway best-seller put all the pieces of biblical prophecy together. Since Jesus had predicted that "this generation" would see the endtimes, he must have been referring to the generation that saw the beginning of the end, which believably was the establishment of the modern state of Israel in 1948. A biblical generation is forty years, so that puts the end at 1988, which means the rapture was scheduled to happen in 1981.

In 1970 that was pretty stunning stuff. The Jesus Movement was in full flower, and people were eager for a new angle on religion. It was also a grim era—Vietnam, inflation, riots, assassinations, political scandals. The time was ripe for a vision of the future that was both bleak and blessed. Yes, the world is going to hell in a handbasket, but you can catch a ride to heaven. People were ready for that message.

Hal Lindsey preached it. A Dallas Seminary grad who had worked with Campus Crusade for eight years, Lindsey wrapped dispensationalist eschatology in the daily papers and came out with an exciting adventure story. He grabbed prophecies from Ezekiel, Daniel, Revelation, and Jesus' sermon on the Mount of Olives and wove them together with modern events to create a compelling scenario. Suddenly obscure references were making sense. The tiny nation of Israel would be the focus of a worldwide conflict. The "Kings of the North," Ezekiel's "Gog and Magog," were obviously Russia. Lindsey cited the growing strength of China as the "Kings of the East" and predicted an army of 200 million marching into war. Europe's Common Market would clearly be the ten-toed feet of Daniel's image, and the Antichrist would arise here. Meanwhile, everyone would have to be tattooed, wrist and forehead, with "the mark of the beast" in order to buy or sell anything.

This was the time of Larry Norman's song "I Wish We'd All Been Ready," and the classic Christian film *A Thief in the Night* was still being widely shown. You didn't want the rapture to happen without you. Of course some Christians got so caught up in Bible prophecy, they didn't care about much else. (We remember one young Christian in 1970 who, seeing headlines about fatal flooding, exclaimed, "Praise the Lord! It's the endtimes!")

The *New York Times* declared that *The Late Great Planet Earth* was the "No. 1 Nonfiction Best-Seller of the Decade," selling more than seven million copies through the bookstores in the 1970s. Ten million copies were in print. This was an exciting new day for Christian publishing. Up until then, a chasm existed between general and evangelical book publishing. But with the publication of Lindsey's book, an evangelical book became a familiar sight in places where it normally would not have been seen before, including general bookstores, supermarkets, and airport newsstands.

Lindsey went on to write other best-sellers like *Satan Is Alive and Well on Planet Earth* (1972). And he did revise *The Late Great Planet Earth*. That 1981 rapture prediction needed an overhaul.

That's the problem with speculative books on Bible prophecy. Earlier in the century it was a matter of guessing if the Antichrist would be Mussolini or Hitler. But the intriguing thing about Bible prophecy is that it always lands on its feet. Maybe there aren't enough "toes" in the European union anymore, but how long before we get our cash cards tattooed on our hands? And prophecies about "the whole world" seeing Christ or the prophets—well, satellite technology and the Internet make this possible in ways only dreamed of in 1970.

Jesus Christ will return some day—no doubt about that—and Bible prophecy will be fulfilled. But between now and then, there will be many more best-selling prophecy "experts" who have guessed wrong.

Eighth Day of Creation

1971

ELIZABETH O'CONNOR

It's a simple enough idea, and it's right there in the Bible. Every Christian has a gift, something to offer the rest of the church, something that works together with other people's gifts to build up the church and glorify God. It's an energizing idea. Imagine: Everybody in your church using some God-given ability to help everyone else. Each person is a minister!

Yet throughout most of church history, this idea was virtually ignored. There were blips of attention here and there, but in America at least, no one paid much mind to spiritual gifts until the late 1960s. It may have come out of the charismatic movement, but the new craze quickly caught on with mainstream evangelicals. "Find Your Spiritual Gift!" It had a gimmicky appeal, something like those self-discovery tests you'd take in *McCall's* or *Good Housekeeping.* Answer a few questions and discover what God wants you to do with your life!

Throughout the seventies it was the hot topic in Christian education, perfectly tailored for this "Me Decade." People were finding out about themselves but then plugging that info back into the church. Everybody won!

Early in this movement, the book *Eighth Day of Creation* came out of The Church of the Saviour in Washington, D.C. It was a cutting-edge church, pioneering efforts in church fellowship and urban ministry (one of a dozen or so experimental urban churches of that time). Elizabeth O'Connor was on staff at the church.

God created the world in six days and rested on the seventh; the eighth day is ours. He has given us gifts to use creatively. In fact, this book is saying, he has given us gifts *for the purpose of creating.* This takes commitment and courage. We also need an environment that encourages us to discover and use our gifts. You might expect O'Connor to give us an outline of the strategies of The Church of the Saviour. She doesn't. Instead, it's a pep talk, an inspirational discussion of the issues underlying the use of our gifts.

Adding inspiration to insight, the last half of the book contains lengthy quotations about creativity and giftedness from a variety of sources—Maslow, Nietszche, Thomas Merton, Martin Buber, among many others. Critics might object to the vagueness of the book. It never lists the spiritual gifts of Scripture. It doesn't offer "Seven Steps to Discovering Your Gift." It just charges you up, points you in a certain direction, gives you a bunch of quotes to munch on, and pushes you out into the wilderness. And yes, that's sort of the point. It's *your* creativity. What are *you* going to do with it?

This book became an important antidote to some of the excesses of the spiritual gifts movement that followed. While some tried to pigeonhole Christians into the seventeen or twenty gifts mentioned in Scripture, O'Connor ignored those restrictions. (Wouldn't a creative God give us ever new ways of creating?) While many used spiritual gifts as a popular method of self-discovery, O'Connor kept the focus on ministry. (It's not what gifts you *have,* but what gifts you *use.*) And while some tried to harness spiritual gifts for church growth or church fellowship, O'Connor broadened the picture with her theology of creativity. We are carrying on God's mission, she was saying, not just redeeming or sanctifying, but *creating.*

The Hiding Place

1971

CORRIE TEN BOOM
with JOHN *and* ELIZABETH SHERRILL

Corrie ten Boom was an unlikely hero, but a hero she certainly was. The humble daughter of a Dutch watchmaker, she stood up against the German Gestapo. She didn't have to do it, and that made it even more remarkable. Some heroes have their circumstances thrust upon them, and in a time of crisis they rise to epic proportions. But Corrie deliberately chose to harbor Jews, defying the Nazis, knowing full well what would happen if she were caught.

The story of Corrie and her sister Betsie, along with Father ten Boom, as told in *The Hiding Place,* has become an enduring Christian classic, precisely because it is the story of an average Christian doing what a Christian should be doing. The book was made into a movie by Worldwide Pictures and it has also been translated into many different languages, making it available around the world. Total sales are in the millions.

When the film *Schindler's List* came out in the 1990s, some began comparing Corrie ten Boom's heroism with that of Otto Schindler. Yet in many ways Corrie's was even more remarkable.

Her story begins with the Dutch prime minister assuring his citizens that the Germans would not attack their peace-loving country. But that night Hitler attacked and suddenly the streets were teeming with German soldiers. In the town of Haarlem, Corrie had operated clubs for girls and for mentally handicapped youth for nearly twenty years. But these she was forced to close down.

When German soldiers ransacked the shop of a Jewish merchant across the street, the ten Booms took him in. Soon other Jews were coming to the ten Boom home, which had several spare rooms. Eventually a secret room was built, a hiding place behind a false wall, into which the Jewish residents were herded when the Nazis came to the door. Eventually, Corrie and Betsie were arrested, along with their aged father, who died ten days later in a jail near The Hague. The sisters were sent to a labor camp in southern Holland and then (after the Allied invasion of Europe) to the Ravensbruck concentration camp, which housed thirty-five thousand women. This was known as "the concentration camp of no return," and it was here that Betsie ten Boom died.

Before Betsie died, however, she had had a vision, and afterwards she told Corrie, "We must tell people how good God is. After the war, we must go around the world telling people. No one will be able to say that they have suffered worse than us. We can tell them how wonderful God is, and how His love will fill our lives, if only we will give up our hatred and bitterness."

During their imprisonment, that is what they did. The ten Booms kept telling others of God's goodness and of salvation in Jesus Christ. Finally, on New Year's Day 1945, under extraordinary circumstances, Corrie was released.

Back in Holland she established a rehabilitation home for victims of concentration camps and a home for refugees on the site of a former concentration camp in Darmstadt. After the war, she became an ambassador of grace and forgiveness around the world, telling people of God's love and goodness, just as Betsie had prophesied.

Corrie wrote more than a dozen books, but her best-seller was *The Hiding Place,* and she used the proceeds to support missionary work. She was already over fifty years old when she was taken to the Nazi concentration camp, and no one would have blamed her for "retiring" after those experiences. But she remained active in her sixties, seventies, and even eighties, telling her story of God's love in the midst of crisis. She died in 1983, at the age of ninety-one.

Evidence That Demands
a Verdict

1972

JOSH McDOWELL

Nowadays many people consider faith a matter of the heart, not the head. They assume Christianity, like other religions, is based on myths and legends, philosophies and fables. Believe whatever you want, they say, just don't try to prove it. { 171 }

In his landmark book, Josh McDowell does just that. He tries to prove the authenticity of Jesus Christ and the Christian faith. And he does a pretty good job.

McDowell isn't the first author to present reasons to believe, but never have they been laid out so thoroughly. He offers support for the Bible from archaeology and fulfilled prophecy. Like a good lawyer he considers the questions of skeptics and puts forth his evidence. This book is most effective in the discussion of Jesus' resurrection, certainly a linchpin of the faith. If Jesus is still dead, McDowell asks, where is the body? Why didn't the Romans produce it? Why didn't the Jewish authorities? And why would Jesus' disciples die for a "fact" they knew to be false?

We must give a nod here to Frank Morison's book *Who Moved the Stone?* (1930), which presented these points years earlier. It should be said that McDowell isn't making up these defenses of the faith, for the most part, but collecting them from various sources. Still, the result is a powerful arsenal of arguments in favor of Christianity.

It's also interesting to compare this work with another similar book—Paul Little's *Know Why You Believe* (1967). The two books have much of the same content, but with different tones. This may reflect the different callings of the two campus ministries these authors have come from. Paul Little was with Inter-Varsity, largely concerned with discipling Christian students, nurturing them in their faith. That's why it's called the Inter-

Varsity Christian *Fellowship*. IV has always been interested in evangelism, but more along the lines of Becky Pippert's *Out of the Saltshaker*—that is, urging Christians to live for Christ and be ready to answer questions about him.

Josh McDowell comes from Campus Crusade for Christ, which has a much more "in your face" attitude toward evangelism. After all, it's a "crusade." This is where the "Four Spiritual Laws" came from. Their calling is to challenge unbelievers to consider the claims of Christ. College students tend to have lots of questions and challenges of their own. A book like *Evidence That Demands a Verdict* meets those challenges. You expect to see Little's book read by a Christian student curled up in a chair by herself, thinking, *I guess my faith really does make sense.* But you'll see McDowell's book in the student union, between a Christian student and the skeptic he's debating, well-thumbed and with a few coffee stains.

The book's logic isn't always airtight. Some arguments are circular, quoting Scripture to prove Scripture. A brilliant skeptic could shoot down a number of these lines of reasoning. But the book keeps coming at you, and the sheer volume of valid evidence is impressive. For the last two decades, when Christians have asked for a book to help them back up what they believe, *Evidence . . .* is what gets recommended.

The Wounded Healer

1972

HENRI NOUWEN

Sometimes the most powerful part of a book is its title. Sometimes that's all you need. *The Wounded Healer* is a tiny book, just a hundred pages, and Nouwen fills these pages with insightful analysis and inspiring stories. But the main gift this book has given the world is the simple idea captured by its title—*The Wounded Healer.*

This is a book for ministers, spiritual healers. These leaders feel enormous pressure to be strong for their people. In times of crisis they must carry everyone else. People look to these ministers for answers. As a result, they often hide their own wounds. They deny their own struggles and doubts.

Nouwen, a Catholic priest involved in ministry to the disabled, understood this double life and urged such leaders to make their wounds a source of healing. How? By using these wounds to connect with the people they serve. This is simple compassion and understanding, yes, but Nouwen calls it *hospitality.* The hospitable host pays attention to a guest, and the wounded healer *concentrates* on those who come for healing. The hospitable host offers a place of *community,* and so the wounded healer creates a company of wounded souls who can share their struggles with one another.

This may seem like common sense to you—now. But in 1972 it was groundbreaking. Now we see support groups and seeker churches and pastors who bare their souls to their congregations. That's Nouwen's influence behind all of those, for good or ill. But in its time, Nouwen's honesty was refreshing. *The Wounded Healer* was a message of liberation for struggling ministers.

We often forget how far-reaching the social revolution of the 1960s was. For a decade, 1964–73, Beatles to Watergate, everything was questioned. Many of society's assumptions were overturned. The hippies' catchphrase "Do your own thing" became a clarion call for personal freedom, a pursuit that is even stronger today. The church had to scramble for effective ways to do ministry in this new era. There were peace protests in the mainline churches and Jesus freaks in California, but the main strategy that made a difference was simple honesty. Don't pretend you have all the answers if you don't. That was the plan Nouwen was proposing.

The Wounded Healer spends three of its four chapters exploring the human condition in the modern age. Many other books at the time were doing this, trying to figure out the new world. Nouwen talks about "the nuclear man," "fragmentation," "historical dislocation," "a generation without fathers." As insightful as those labels are, Nouwen wasn't alone in applying them. But the fourth chapter of this little book carries the payload: ". . . a deep understanding of his [the minister's] own pain makes it possible for him to convert his weakness into strength and to offer his own experience as a source of healing to those who are often lost in the darkness of their own misunderstood sufferings."

In other words, the wounded minister becomes a healer.

The Total Woman

1973

MARABEL MORGAN

For four straight years the top-selling book in the United States was a Christian book. In two of those years it was *The Living Bible;* in another year it was Billy Graham's *Angels: God's Secret Agents.* In the fourth year, it was a book written by a Miami housewife.

Today the shelves in Christian bookstores are filled with books on marriage, but in the early 1970s that wasn't true. Cecil Osborne's *The Art of Understanding Your Mate* and Tim LaHaye's *How to Be Happy though Married* were exceptions.

But Marabel Morgan wanted to do something for women by a woman and she had the right credentials. The wife of an attorney and the mother of two daughters, she had started a marriage enrichment program in south Florida called Total Woman. It had become so successful that she needed several other instructors to help her teach the burgeoning program.

As the *Miami Herald* reported, "Word spread from one friend to another. Marabel became the Ann Landers of her set. Soon the women were gathering in groups to listen and learn. Among the graduates are Anita Bryant and enough football wives to read like a Dolphins roster."

On the Phil Donahue TV show, Morgan's appearance received one of the most impressive responses the show ever had. The *National Enquirer* reviewed her plan and played it straight: "The Total Woman concept is a how-to course, not only meant for marriages in deep trouble but for women who have fine marriages and want to make them finer." The *Sun Tattler* commented: "The course concerns how not to ask for things, how to communicate when you are irritated, understanding the differences between men and women, and how each approaches a situation from an entirely different premise."

It was only because Marabel's own marriage was in the doldrums that she started to think and read and discover how to put the sizzle back into her married life. "The results of applying certain principles to my marriage were so revolutionary that I had to pass them on in the four-lesson Total Woman course, and now in this book."

In a nutshell, the four lessons are (1) get organized, (2) accept and appreciate your husband, (3) work on your sex life, and (4) learn the secrets of good communication. She wrote: "This book is not intended to be the ultimate authority on marriage. Far from it. I don't pretend to have an automatic, ready-to-wear answer for every marriage problem. I do believe it is possible, however, for almost any wife to have her husband absolutely adore her in just a few weeks' time. She can revive romance, reestablish communication, break down barriers, and put sizzle back into her marriage. It really is up to her. She has the power."

When the mass-market edition of the book began to sell, sales shot into the millions. The book had its critics, and some said that it would appeal to women of the previous generation rather than to women of the 1970s, but that didn't seem to hinder its popularity. The book was also one of the earlier "crossover" books in Christian publishing, where sales are stronger in the secular market than in Christian bookstores. Although the religious aspect is not strong through most of the book, Morgan ends up with a chapter called "Power Source," in which she shares her own personal testimony.

So *Total Woman* opened the door to more practical books on marriage, more crossover books, and more books by women that display disarming honesty, have touches of humor, and are intensely helpful.

Knowing God

1973

J. I. PACKER

Nothing is as important as knowing God. It is, says J. I. Packer, "the most practical project anyone can engage in." In fact "we are cruel to ourselves if we try to live in this world without knowing about the God whose world it is and who runs it." But {177} knowledge about God is not the same as knowing God personally. Looking back at the psalmist, Packer says, "the psalmist's concern to get knowledge about God was not a theoretical, but a practical concern. His supreme desire was to know and enjoy God himself, and he valued knowledge about God simply as a means to this end."

As a theologian, Packer stands as one of the most influential thinkers and apologists for Christianity in the twentieth century. His writings have a concern for clarity, logic, and practicality.

Raised in a working-class family in Gloucester, England, he had few thoughts about God or religion until a Unitarian friend got him thinking more deeply. But as he entered college, all he really cared about was jazz. (He played a mean clarinet in a jazz band called the Oxford Bandits.) But he promised a friend that he'd attend some services of the Oxford Inter-Collegiate Christian Union, and he described it later in terms reminiscent of the apostle Paul's conversion: "the scales fell from my eyes." It was, he says, "an ordinary conversion," but it certainly started an extraordinary career.

Packer served as a curate of a Birmingham, England, church for three years, before returning to the academic world at Tyndale Hall, Bristol. There he wrote his first book, *Fundamentalism and the Word of God* (1958), which grabbed the attention of the evangelical public and established his reputation. While Packer distanced himself from an anti-intellectual position of many fundamentalists of the time, he proudly claimed the label *evangelical* (actually he preferred the term *historic* evangelical). Liberalism, he said, was totally subjective, based entirely on human reason and analysis, while evangelicalism was "nothing but Christianity itself."

In 1973 *Knowing God* was published. Originally it had been a series of magazine articles for a British magazine, and so it was slanted to a lay audience. Most of the articles dealt with the attributes of God, but Packer went on to outline the implications of these doctrines in everyday life. So the book became a kind of applied theology.

Obviously, it hit the mark. Within ten years it had sold a half million copies, and within twenty years it had sold more than a million copies in English alone. Translations were also published in French, German, Korean, Chinese, Japanese, Spanish, Norwegian, Finnish, Polish, and modern Hebrew. For many readers it was the first "theology" book they had read in their lives.

In his final chapter, Packer states his aim: "We set out to see what it means to know God. We found that the God who is 'there' for us to know is the God of the Bible, the God of Romans, the God revealed in Jesus, the Three-in-One of historic Christian teaching. We realized that knowing him starts with knowing about him, so we studied his revealed character and ways and came to know something of his goodness and severity, his wrath and his grace. As we did so, we learned to re-evaluate ourselves as fallen creatures, not strong and self-sufficient as we once supposed, but weak, foolish and indeed bad, heading not for Utopia but for hell unless grace intervenes. Also, we saw that knowing God involves a personal relationship whereby you give yourself to God on the basis of his promise to give himself to you. . . . Now finally, we learn that a man who knows God will be more than conqueror . . . exulting with Paul in the adequacy of God."

In 1979 Packer became professor of historical and systematic theology at Regent College in Vancouver, British Columbia, and he went on to do more writing—including *Keep in Step with the Spirit* and *Rediscovering Holiness*. Roger Nicole, an eminent theologian himself, comments, "Surely if soundness is considered as a paramount qualification for a theologian, Packer must be numbered among the greatest theologians of our generation."

The Gulag Archipelago

1973

ALEKSANDR SOLZHENITSYN

Sometimes a book is more than its words and ideas. Sometimes it's an event, an artifact, a symbol. *The Gulag Archipelago* is like that, a triumph of truth over repression, the indomitable testimony of a man who found faith within the Soviet system of *gulags,* or prison camps.

In the USSR, information was a hot commodity. The state tried to control its flow, preventing citizens from criticizing their leaders or conditions in the country. As a result, the penal system remained mysterious—each *gulag* an island isolated from its surroundings. The collection of these "islands" could be considered a kind of lost continent—a *gulag* archipelago—unknown to the outside world.

It was a crime of information that got Aleksandr Solzhenitsyn into the *gulag,* and a triumph of information that later kept him out. As a twenty-seven-year-old captain in the Soviet army, he was arrested in 1945 for making remarks critical of Stalin in a letter to a friend. That earned him eight years in labor camps. Though he began his military career as a devoted Marxist, these events turned him against the authorities. He fought back with the only weapon he had—information. In each *gulag* he gathered the stories of inmates, conditions, leaders, and the history of those facilities.

Released in 1953 because of his terminal cancer (from which he later recovered), he taught high school physics and mathematics—but he also wrote. His novels *One Day in the Life of Ivan Denisovich* (1962) and *The First Circle* (1968) are both set in Soviet prison camps. But he was still working on something larger, a nonfiction collection of accounts from the prison camps. The stories needed to be told, but Solzhenitsyn feared that publishing such a book would endanger some of his friends from the *gulag,* so he held back the manuscript. "My obligation to those still living outweighed my obligation to the dead," he wrote. Only when government agents began seizing his papers did he feel the need to rush the book to print in the Western world. Volume 1 of *The Gulag Archipelago* came out in 1973, first in some installments in the *New York Times* and then in book form.

It was a worldwide sensation, light from a dark cave, word from a lost continent. Those inmates who had vanished from their communities were suddenly very visible. The institutionalized injustice of the entire *gulag* system was exposed. Of course the Soviet government was embarrassed to see their dirty laundry waved about like this, but what could they do? To send Solzhenitsyn back to the *gulag* would just confirm all his criticism. He was a worldwide celebrity now, so they had to treat him right.

Their solution was banishment. So in 1974 Solzhenitsyn headed west, first to Zurich and later to Vermont, living a rather reclusive life. Though various groups tried to use him for their own purposes, he didn't allow himself to be used. And his criticism has lashed out against the materialism and secularism of the Western world, just as it had attacked the Soviet system. In 1994 he returned to live in Russia.

Solzhenitsyn's masterwork was a courageous achievement and a significant event in the ongoing global conflict between Communism and democracy. But for Christians it has special significance, because Solzhenitsyn found faith during his *gulag* experience. He'd been deeply affected by some Christian inmates he encountered along the way. Somehow they could have joy in the midst of suffering, love in the midst of injustice. Solzhenitsyn put their stories in his book.

And so Christians could see this as a triumph of a special kind of information, the good news of Jesus Christ. Solzhenitsyn reminded us of the struggles of Christians in the USSR, in China, and in other oppressive regimes, but he also gave us hope. Even in a powerful system that denies God's existence, committing itself to demeaning and destroying people, the truth cannot be squelched.

All We're Meant to Be

1974

LETHA SCANZONI
and NANCY HARDESTY

"Women's liberation" was big news in the early 1970s. That's what they called it then, not yet the more academic "feminism." Writers such as Betty Friedan and Gloria Steinem announced that women had been enslaved by society, and it was time to break those chains. The Equal Rights Amendment was passed by Congress in 1972 and began its circuit through the states, seeking ratification. Some saw the 1973 *Roe v. Wade* decision on abortion as a victory for women's rights. Many began to wonder why talented women were kept out of leadership positions in business, government, and even the church. As with any social movement, some protesters went to extremes. But there were many sober-minded people of both sexes carefully examining the fairest way to go. And that included a number of Christians.

Evangelical churches generally reserved leadership roles for men. Women could run the children's program, support the church in a ladies' auxiliary, and perform music in church services. (They could also do virtually anything on the mission field.) But pastors were men, as were the key chairmen and Bible teachers. This arrangement (which a number of churches still follow) was based on a handful of Bible passages. But there had been little discussion about the best interpretation of those passages. It was often assumed that, because the husband was the "head" of the wife, any man should have authority over any woman in the church. Or that, because Adam was created first, men were closer to God.

Enter Scanzoni—a sociology professor specializing in marriage and the family—and Hardesty—a journalist-turned-scholar with an emphasis in church history. *All We're Meant to Be* made a strong case for a new view of women within the church and in Christian homes. The strength of the book was in its biblical orientation. Subtitled *A Biblical Approach to Women's Liberation*, this book discussed the pertinent passages with respect and insight. The public was used to screeds from secular feminists decrying the old ways, but *All We're Meant to Be* was positioned squarely within the Bible-believing church. It was published by Word. The authors connected when Hardesty edited a Scanzoni article for *Eternity*, a well-respected evangelical magazine. They weren't saying, "Ignore the Bible." They were saying, "Understand it."

And Scanzoni and Hardesty saw the Bible as a liberating document. Adam and Eve were created as partners. They sinned together and were cursed together. Jesus treated women with respect that was astonishing for his day. At Pentecost Peter quoted Joel's prophecy that "your sons *and daughters* shall prophesy"—and in fact the New Testament and early church history show us a number of Christian women breaking their cultural bonds and taking leadership roles alongside men in the church's ministry.

{ 182 }

Christian readers were rightly on guard against the male-bashing, marriage-destroying, ladder-climbing rhetoric they had been hearing from early advocates of women's lib. But that's not what they got in this book. Christian women in particular understood that leadership in Jesus' eyes was not about power or prestige, but service, so they resisted the language of self-exaltation. But Scanzoni and Hardesty made an impassioned plea for the full use of women's gifts *in the service of the church*. Their title made their point: They were merely asking that Christian women be allowed to be all they were meant (by God) to be.

The book was certainly controversial. Many disagreed with its interpretation of Scripture and distrusted its intentions. Some feared that it would just carry the church along with the worldly tide of feminism. But many other Christians found a voice in this book. Many women, frustrated with the church's neglect of their gifts but fearing that they were being unspiritual by complaining, gained new confidence. Men and women began to study this subject in Scripture with new eyes.

And many churches have changed during the quarter century since this influential book appeared. Many women are pastors in mainline denominations, and even some of the more evangelical churches and denominations have gifted women on their pastoral staffs or leadership teams. In general, the gifts of women are respected and welcomed more than ever.

It's possible that the church would have come to this point anyway, just rolling along with the changes in the culture. But the main contribution of Scanzoni and Hardesty's book is this: The church has made these changes *because* of what the Bible says and not *in spite of* it.

Born Again

1976

CHARLES COLSON

The church has often drawn great benefit from unlikely converts. The apostle Paul persecuted Christians before he saw the light. Saint Augustine was an ambitious playboy. John Newton was a slave trader before he was converted and penned "Amazing Grace." In our day there's Chuck Colson, famous as a "hatchet man" in the Nixon White House, convicted in the Watergate cover-up.

Colson's testimony fills his first book, *Born Again.* Watergate was one of the biggest stories of the century, and this was one of the first memoirs of the participants to be published. A curious public snapped up the book—and got more than it bargained for. This was more than a confession of political crimes; it was a tale of personal transformation.

As the Watergate scandal was unfolding in the press, a different drama was unfolding in Chuck Colson's heart. A friend challenged him to consider the claims of Christ, giving him a copy of C. S. Lewis's *Mere Christianity.* Colson's fine-tuned legal mind appreciated Lewis's logical arguments, but it took a while to convince him. He began writing his questions on legal pads, poring through Scripture and Lewis for answers. Eventually he gave his heart to Christ. This was no jailhouse repentance, no conversion of convenience. Colson was just beginning to plunge into the whirlpool of the Watergate hearings at the time. He quietly met with a prayer group of Christians in Congress and grew in his faith. When he was convicted, he did his time in prison (an experience that later inspired him to establish Prison Fellowship, one of the most effective Christian ministries of our time). And when he wrote *Born Again,* he made it clear that it was not the Nixon exposé everyone was hungry for but the story of one man's needy life and the Savior who met that need.

By the way, it was this book, along with President Carter's open spirituality, that launched the "born-again chic" of the late 1970s. Jesus used the phrase "born again" once, but twentieth-century evangelicals had adopted it as a kind of code word. Emphasizing the need for a personal decision to follow Christ, evangelicals had to distinguish themselves from the many "nominal" or "cultural" Christians in the world. If you asked, "Are you a Christian?" most Americans would say yes, based on church membership or childhood baptism. But the question "Are you born again?" separated the sheep from the goats.

But it remained a secret handshake until Colson and Carter went public with the term. Suddenly everyone was talking about being born again and the phrase suffered major dilution. Madison Avenue hijacked the words. Pop music borrowed them. Any new experience—jogging, perfume, sex—could make you feel "born again."

The fad faded, and the phrase returned to its previous owners, only now it had a pejorative sense. The secular world used the label "born again" for a sociopolitical bloc of conservative evangelical-fundamentalists who were considered ignorant, obnoxious, and judgmental. By the 1990s, when asked by unchurched neighbors if they were "born again," some evangelicals were responding, "Well, yes, but not in the way you think."

Certainly we can't blame Colson for the ups and downs of his book title, but it's a part of the major influence he has had. Fortunately Colson himself was no fad. We had seen several other flash-in-the-pan converts, but this man proved his sincerity in the following decades. Besides his work at the helm of Prison Fellowship, Chuck Colson also became a leading thinker in evangelicalism. He wouldn't claim to be a theologian but he surrounded himself with experts and learned from them. Then he would communicate his learning with the masses in his radio spots, newsletter, *Christianity Today* column, and a host of books. *Loving God, Kingdoms in Conflict, The Body, Who Speaks for God?, How Now Shall We Live?*—all of these works touched on the responsibility of Christians toward God, toward one another, and to the world around them.

In a way, Colson has been answering the questions Francis Schaeffer asked, and in language that people could understand. Colson has always promoted personal devotion but he always traces its implications out into society. He wants Christians to think about how they live and then to live according to what they believe. He's still a political creature, so he doesn't shy away from political analysis. Some Christians might disagree with his positions (though you might brand him a "compassionate conservative"), but you have to appreciate the thinking that gets him there. This is no knee-jerk commentator; Colson raises the level of any debate. You may disagree with his conclusions but you'd better come prepared to support your views.

Born Again stands as the firstfruits of an impressive output from this unlikely convert. It would be hard to find another communicator in the last quarter of the century who has had as much influence on the church as this onetime White House lawyer.

Joni

1976

JONI EARECKSON
with JOE MUSSER

In 1975 on the *Today* show, Barbara Walters interviewed a quadriplegic who had learned to draw while holding a pen with her teeth. Eight years earlier, at the age of seventeen, Joni (pronounced "Johnny") Eareckson broke her neck and became paralyzed when she dived into the Chesapeake Bay. She told Barbara Walters that she had been able to rebuild her life and accept her incurable condition because of her faith in Jesus Christ.

Zondervan Publishing House contacted her shortly thereafter, and the following year an autobiography was published with a dust jacket showing her drawing with a pen in her mouth, and the title simply *Joni.* Within a few years, more than two million copies of her book were sold, and in 1980 the film *Joni* was released by Worldwide Pictures. She soon was making frequent appearances at Billy Graham crusades. *Time* magazine did a full-page story on her in the 1980 end-of-the-year issue. Even her artwork was much in demand.

Capitalizing on her growing prominence, Joni started a ministry to the handicapped called Joni and Friends in 1979, which she continues to operate out of her California headquarters. A second book, *A Step Beyond,* which delves into the problem of suffering from a biblical as well as a personal standpoint, passed the one million mark in sales very quickly. More books came from Joni in the 1980s and 1990s—she has now written more than twenty—making her a very significant author of the latter part of the century.

Several of Joni's books have heightened awareness of the handicapped. And in addition to her writing, her ministry trains local churches for effective outreach to the handicapped. Joni and Friends has now gone international, with a presence in twenty European countries as well as in Latin America and Asia. She also records a five-minute radio program heard daily on more than seven hundred radio stations. By presidential appointment Joni served on the National Council for Disability, and during her time on the commission, the Americans for Disabilities Act became law. All this began with the book titled *Joni*.

The book begins with a quotation from the Phillips paraphrase of 2 Corinthians 4:8; "We are handicapped on all sides, but we are never frustrated; we are puzzled, but never in despair." She had become a Christian only two years before the accident but was discouraged by her lack of spiritual progress in those years. "Please do something in my life," she had prayed shortly before her accident, "to turn it around."

While in her hospital bed, she experienced the range of emotions from confidence that God would somehow heal her, to despair and asking for a quick death. "Slowly I became aware of God's interest in me. I was some sort of 'cosmic guinea pig'—a representative of the human race on whom truth could be tested. All the distractions, trappings, and things were gone. God had taken them away and had placed me here without distractions. My life was reduced to absolute basics. So now what? What am I to do with my life? I wondered. I have no body, but I am still someone. I had to find meaning, purpose, and direction, not just some measure of temporary satisfaction."

Her honesty in expressing her emotions in the book has helped thousands of others with various disabilities realize that they are not alone.

A friend, Steve Estes, helped her gain insight as she struggled with her paralysis. Once he told her, "Joni, your body . . . is only the frame for God's portrait of you. Y'know, people don't go to an art gallery to admire frames. Their focus is on the quality and character of the paintings." That gave her a new perspective.

Gradually, she found opportunities for ministry. A Baltimore newspaper columnist once asked her why she signed her paintings "PTL," and she explained that it meant "Praise the Lord." She went on to say, "My art is a reflection of how God can empower someone like me to rise above circumstances."

The Battle for the Bible

1976

HAROLD LINDSELL

For longtime evangelical leaders like Harold Lindsell, it must have felt like déjà vu. J. I. Packer had expressed his concern in *Fundamentalism and the Word of God*. Francis Schaeffer, at the {189} Congress on World Evangelism in 1974, predicted that the "crucial area of discussion for evangelicalism in the next several years will be Scripture. At stake is whether evangelicalism will remain evangelical." He said that there was no use in evangelicalism getting bigger "if at the same time appreciable parts of evangelicalism are getting soft at the central core, namely the Scriptures." About the same time Packer, R. C. Sproul, and James Montgomery Boice were planning a conference for the defense of the inerrancy of Scripture.

So the time was right for Harold Lindsell's book.

He and others of the older generation of evangelicals remembered the struggle that had gone on in the early part of the century. Theologian B. B. Warfield had spelled out the doctrine of the inerrancy of Scripture back in 1881, and that view was quoted often by fundamentalist leaders in the first thirty years of the twentieth century. Liberals had not only denied historic Christian doctrines, they charged, but had rejected the notion of a reliable biblical record.

Out of that turmoil the fundamentalist movement had emerged, and then gradually the rough edges of fundamentalism were smoothed into evangelicalism—which sought to be less cantankerous, more reasonable, less separatist, and more with it. In that spirit, a score of vital new movements and missions sprang up in the 1940s and 1950s. Doctrinally they upheld the same basic doctrines as the fundamentalists: the inspiration of Scripture, the virgin birth, the atoning death of Christ, his bodily resurrection, and the blessed hope of the second coming.

But now Lindsell and others—many of whom had been active in the rise of evangelicalism—were seeing a waffling on the inerrancy of Scripture. And Lindsell, Francis Schaeffer, and J. I. Packer were saying, "Oh, no! Here we go again!"

A former professor at Fuller Theological Seminary and at this time editor of the prestigious *Christianity Today* magazine, Lindsell examined all the foxholes and fired shots wherever he sensed any movement away from a tight inerrancy position.

After defining the problem, showing how Scripture talks of its own infallibility and outlining how the doctrine was considered throughout church history, Lindsell points out the defections he had noticed in the Lutheran Church—Missouri Synod, the Southern Baptist Convention, and Fuller Theological Seminary, where he had previously taught. He mentions examples of slippage in evangelical parachurch organizations, as well as in some smaller evangelical denominations. He then takes a chapter to discuss how alleged discrepancies in Scripture can be handled. In conclusion, he reemphasizes, "Errancy leads to further concessions." Consequently, to evangelicals who believed as he did, "I urge you to contend earnestly for the faith. . . . I urge you to take whatever action is needed to secure a redress of the situation."

Lindsell began his preface by saying, "I regard the subject of the book, biblical inerrancy, to be the most important theological topic of the age." Other key leaders agreed. John Walvoord of Dallas Theological Seminary called Lindsell's effort "one of the most strategic books to be published by evangelicals." Harold John Ockenga, one of the founders of the National Association of Evangelicals in 1942, praised the book's importance, saying, "Those who surrender the doctrine of inerrancy inevitably move away from orthodoxy."

Partly as a result of this book, conservatives in the Southern Baptist Convention began their takeover of the denominational seminaries and headquarters. But many others felt that Lindsell's book was too black-and-white, too quick to draw battle lines. Inerrancy needs to be further defined in a scientific age, some were suggesting. A number of evangelicals preferred a softer definition of inerrancy, such as: "*For the purposes for which the Bible was given,* it is fully truthful and inerrant."

But there was no doubt—whether you loved it or hated it—Lindsell's book left its mark on the evangelical scene for the rest of the century.

Rich Christians
in an Age of Hunger

1977

RON SIDER

Ron Sider is the kind of guy people don't like to have around.
Nothing personal. He's actually a very sweet, soft-spoken gen-
tleman, but his writings pull the rug out from under us.

The logic is pretty simple. If Christians are called to follow
the example of Christ in sacrificial love, and if we have more
material possessions than we need, why aren't we doing all we
can to help the starving people of the world? Sider's book made
a powerful case in 1977, and revised editions are still making
the case.

Of course, Sider didn't invent this idea. You can find it in
1 John 3:17: "If anyone has material possessions and sees his
brother in need but has no pity on him, how can the love of
God be in him?" (NIV). If you think Sider is overstating his case,
at least he's in good company. The book of James also chimes
in: "Suppose a brother or sister is without clothes and daily food.
If one of you says to him, 'Go, I wish you well; keep warm and
well fed,' but does nothing about his physical needs, what good
is it?" (James 2:15–16 NIV).

Ron Sider has had plenty of critics. He's been called simplistic, liberal, even Communist. Some think he's against the idea
of private property. One opponent even published a counter-
attack: *Productive Christians in an Age of Guilt-Manipulators*. (Of
course, if you count Sider among the guilt-manipulators, don't
you have to include James and John as well?)

All right, maybe Sider has been a bit simplistic. He's certainly
coming from that old Anabaptist belief in simple living, and
that may not play very well to Calvinists reared on a Puritan
work ethic. Critics remind us that the problem of world hunger
is complex. We can't just throw money at it and expect it to go

away. There are social, cultural, and political issues involved. Food sent to Somalia can be pirated by warlords. Money can be siphoned off in bribes. Grain can rot on loading docks. But the sad fact remains that most First World Christians don't really care about hunger in the Third World. We allow the complexities to shield us from our responsibility. If we convince ourselves that there really are no workable solutions, then we don't feel so bad about not trying to help.

Rich Christians in an Age of Hunger shoots those defenses down. Sider presents specific ways of helping. These proposals may not all work, but still, we can no longer hide behind the impossibility of the challenge. (And, to Sider's credit, recent editions have tackled more of the complexities as well as updating the statistics.) The good news is that hunger is less of a problem than when this book first came out. But the grim truth, Sider says, is that thirty-four thousand children are still dying each day of starvation and preventable diseases.

A Bible professor at Eastern Baptist Seminary, Sider served as the economic conscience of evangelicals at a crucial time. When it first appeared in 1977, this book clicked with the children of the sixties, recent college grads who were beginning to build their lives and choose their lifestyles. They shared its idealism. Of course our society hurtled into the "Greed is good" eighties and the cyberbooming nineties. Now our churches are filled with "rich Christians" and we're rather jaded about the poverty of the world. We may need to hear Sider's message again.

Celebration of Discipline

1978

RICHARD J. FOSTER

You can say a lot of things about the ills of the modern world. People are selfish, lustful, lacking self-control. The world is violent, pandering, greedy. But perhaps the most important diagnosis is that people are *shallow*. We have learned to define reality in two dimensions, accepting only what we see on a screen—a movie screen, a TV screen, a computer monitor. We judge others by how they look rather than how they act, by how they talk rather than what they say, by what they drive rather than what they dream.

And you would think that Christians would be different. Some are. But far too many of us share in that shallowness. We worship rock stars who happen to sing about God. Like our neighbors, we long for more money, though we do give some of it to the church. We design our church programs so the beautiful people will want to come, attracting other beautiful people. We have a vague sense that there's something wrong with all our attention to the surface of things but we lack the spiritual resources to do anything about it. We just don't have the depth.

That's the problem Richard Foster tackles in *Celebration of Discipline*. "Superficiality is the curse of our age," he begins. That "age" was the 1970s, the era of discos and *Charlie's Angels*. The back-to-basics enthusiasm of the late sixties had faded and we were solidly in the "Me Decade." Other than the hairstyles, not much has changed since then. Foster's words still ring true at the birth of the new millennium: "The desperate need today is not for a greater number of intelligent people, or gifted people, but for deep people."

But Foster wasn't just a voice complaining in the wilderness. He had a plan. *How* do people grow deeper? By recovering the traditional spiritual disciplines of the church.

For evangelicals, this was edgy stuff. Oh, we had no problem with disciplines like prayer and Bible study. Our shelves were packed with books urging us in those directions. But Foster was also talking about meditation, fasting, solitude, submission, and spiritual guidance. He was plumbing the depths of not only his own Quaker background but also the rest of a church history chock full of monks and mystics. This scared some potential readers but it excited many others. In just over two decades, his book has sold a million copies.

Richard Foster has quietly challenged Christians in other books as well. His *Freedom of Simplicity* (1981) recommends a lifestyle less encumbered by consumerism. *Money, Sex and Power* (1985) got some flak for its bold title but it pointedly addressed the three main idolatries of our culture. More recently *Prayer: Finding the Heart's True Home* (1992) was named *Christianity Today's* book of the year. In his books, and in his work with Renovaré, the church renewal ministry he founded, Foster is committed to helping Christians dodge the darts of the world and live as close to Christ as they possibly can.

Foster's books always get great buzz among church people, but none have had the impact of *Celebration of Discipline*. This has been a life-changer. In it Foster divides the spiritual disciplines into three categories. The *inward* disciplines include meditation, prayer, fasting, and study. The *outward* disciplines are simplicity, solitude, submission, and service. Then there are the *corporate* disciplines, which the church practices together—confession, worship, guidance, and celebration.

But Foster does far more than just present the idea of these disciplines. This is a how-to book, giving practical steps for practicing these disciplines. He uses examples from his own life and others' to illustrate his points. In the process, however, he makes it very clear that this is not a new legalism. No one is earning salvation by being devout. This is simply a path to a deepening spirituality, a growing awareness of Christ in all the nooks and crannies of life. Many Christians have followed Foster down that path and are deeply grateful.

Telling the Truth

1979

FREDERICK BUECHNER

Frederick Buechner is a teacher of preachers. His influence on the church of the twentieth century is a two-step process. Many of the common folk of the church have no idea who he is; they can't even pronounce his name (it rhymes with *seeker,* sort of). But chances are, their pastors have been inspired by Buechner's prose, and his words help them tell their people the truth about God.

As a writer, Buechner seems to live two lives. In one of them, he has enjoyed some success as a novelist in the secular market. His fiction blends John Updike and Flannery O'Connor, New England soul-searching and down-home oddities. His four-part serial *The Book of Bebb* both bothers and blesses the Christian reader with its seriously flawed hero, the preacher Leo Bebb. You're not likely to find another story of redemption that grabs your guts like this one.

Buechner the novelist has also dabbled in historical fiction with *Godric* and *Brendan* and even biblical fiction with *Son of Laughter,* Jacob's story. (The conniving patriarch who wrestles with God is Buechner's kind of hero.) In all of his novels, Buechner is at his best describing the inner conflicts of his characters—those wrestling matches with God. He is keenly aware of human foibles and our constant need of God's grace.

But the primary influence of Frederick Buechner on the church has come through his various books of theological essays, sermons, inspirational remembrances, and collections of wit and wisdom. His humor and slightly cynical tone resonate with pastors and church leaders. As a preacher himself, he knows the territory. But this isn't just entertainment: Buechner helps his preacher/readers understand what they do for a living.

Books like *The Alphabet of Grace, Whistling in the Dark,* and *Wishful Thinking* offer short definitions of various subjects (some theological), always with humor, but often with valuable insight. On the boldness of praying the Lord's Prayer, he writes in *Whistling in the Dark*, "To speak those words is to invite the tiger out of the cage, to unleash a power that makes atomic power look like a warm breeze. . . . It is only the words 'Our Father' that make the prayer bearable. If God is indeed something like a father, then as something like children maybe we can risk approaching him anyway."

We select *Telling the Truth* for our list because it speaks most clearly about what preachers do, and thus it represents Buechner's primary influence. Subtitled *The Gospel as Tragedy, Comedy, and Fairy Tale*, this slim volume reminds preachers that they're really just delivering the news—the bad news of sin first, but then the glorious good news of redemption. Don't let the "fairy tale" worry you. He's not saying the gospel is untrue—on the contrary! It's about the huge issues of good and evil that affect all of us. "To preach the Gospel in its original power and mystery," Buechner writes, "is to claim . . . that once upon a time is this time, now." This novelist's skill as a wordsmith and a creator comes into play here, in a work that is deeply inspiring. A seminarian won't find many homiletics texts like this one.

"The task of the preacher is to hold up life to us; by whatever gifts he or she has of imagination, eloquence, simple candor, to create images of life through which we can somehow see into the wordless truth of our lives." Using his own artistic gifts, Frederick Buechner has empowered a few generations of Christian preachers to proclaim the good news with power and beauty.

Where Does a Mother Go to Resign?

1979

BARBARA JOHNSON

Barbara Johnson's books symbolize two trends in Christian publishing: first, books for women; second, humor. Since the mid-1970s women have been the dominant buyers of Christian books; since the mid-1980s many women authors have used humor to get across their message. Barbara Johnson was at the forefront of both trends. { 197 }

Both themes may seem a bit strange when you know the Barbara Johnson story. She's been shaped by experiences with the men in her life, and all these experiences have been traumatically tragic. But because she had gone through so much hardship, she was in a perfect position to help other women, and in 1978 she and her husband, Bill, began Spatula Ministries to help "scrape people off the ceiling"—as in "hitting the ceiling" when you hear shocking news. "Specifically, we pull them off with a spatula of love."

Since her first book, *Where Does a Mother Go to Resign?*, Johnson has written several others, such as *Fresh Elastic for Stretched-Out Moms* and *Stick a Geranium in Your Hat and Be Happy*. Her books regularly hit the best-seller lists now, with total sales well over two million.

Known as an effective women's speaker as well as a writer, Johnson weaves together hilarity and pathos. In *100 Christian Women Who Changed the Twentieth Century,* Helen Hosier puts it this way: "Barbara Johnson is giving a speech punctuated with sidesplitting humor—a Johnson hallmark. The audience cracks up laughing until they have to dab the corners of their eyes. . . . Then she weaves the story of her life and the heart-wrenching family tragedies for which she's known. She has one of the biggest, warmest hearts you'll ever find, and from it overflows joy so radiant you are caught up in it . . . and so she scatters that joy into people's lives and tells them they can do the same. Then she tells them how this can happen, even when they've been overwhelmed by experiences that have all but knocked the very breath out of them."

The first family tragedy that Johnson talks about was the car accident in 1966 that almost took her husband's life. He was left severely brain damaged, and for a while was completely "broken and shattered—physically and mentally." It was then, she says, "we learned that God delights in touching broken people and making them whole. God performed a miracle."

Two years later, they received word that their eighteen-year-old son, Steve, had been killed near Da Nang, Vietnam. He had been overseas with the Marines only four months. As they were emerging from that trauma, their son Tim, returning from a summer of work in Alaska, was killed by a drunk driver. Then a few years later, another shock. Barbara walked into the bedroom of their son Larry and found a stack of homosexual magazines. They had no idea that he was gay. "He was a Christian, active in church and Bible study . . . a model kid, no problems, and popular with girls. These magazines couldn't possibly be his." But they were, and this situation was more difficult for her to accept than the deaths of her two other sons.

That's when she and her husband started Spatula Ministries, to help men and women, but mostly women, whose lives have been broken by similar situations. Much of her work with this caring ministry involves writing or calling parents in crisis. "There are so many hurting people out there, all wanting instant relief. But we know there is no microwave maturity, only a slow growth process."

Since 1996 Johnson has been traveling to major women's conferences, helping women find "the joy of the Lord" despite their circumstances. And if Barbara Johnson could find that joy amid all her heartbreaking experiences, it is certainly available to anyone.

Out of the Saltshaker and into the World

1979

REBECCA MANLEY PIPPERT

Evangelical Christians had painted themselves into a corner. The old fundamentalism had emphasized personal holiness and separation from the world, and thus the first half of this century saw a gradual retreat from "worldly" activities. But the new evangelical movement, coming of age in the 1950s, was hawking the good news of Christianity. Mission societies and youth organizations sprang up, and Billy Graham was making headlines. We began to see how important it was to evangelize.

But how do you evangelize people from whom you've separated yourself? It's not easy. Christians became adept at techniques that resembled dive-bombing. We would hand out tracts to strangers, start random conversations at the beach, or knock on the doors of the neighbors we'd been ignoring, just to tell them that God loved them and had a wonderful plan for their lives.

Techniques of evangelism were plentiful. "Saturation Evangelism." "The Four Spiritual Laws." "Evangelism Explosion." Nothing wrong with these resources, but there was something missing. Personal evangelism wasn't very personal.

Becky Pippert changed that. *Out of the Saltshaker* called Christians to get beyond the techniques and just be themselves. "I believe that much of our evangelism is ineffective because we depend too much upon technique and strategy," Pippert wrote in her preface. "Evangelism has slipped into the sales department. I am convinced that we must look at Jesus, and the quality of life he calls us to, as a model for . . . how to reach out to others."

We are the "salt of the earth," Jesus said. Pippert was urging Christians to escape from their cloisters and establish "salty" relationships with people who need God's love. Jesus loved people, listened to them, and touched their lives. We should do the same. There's no place for dive-bombing, Pippert was saying. Incarnational evangelism demands that we share *ourselves* with people, not just our words.

Rebecca Manley Pippert wasn't the first to promote "lifestyle evangelism," nor was she the last, but she made her case in such a winsome way that she won many fans. Some traditionalists feared that this new approach let Christians off the hook, that it endorsed a "silent witness," which was no witness at all. But Pippert's challenge came not from skepticism, but from a deep desire to win souls. A staffer with InterVarsity Christian Fellowship, she was obviously committed to evangelism—she just wanted to see it done right, rooted in relationships rather than formulas.

A generation of Christians took her words to heart. Youth and college ministries, mission organizations, and churches began putting more emphasis on relationship-based evangelism. When Christians get out of the saltshaker and start seasoning their communities, then the good news is truly good.

With Justice for All

1982

JOHN PERKINS

In the 1800s evangelical Christians led the way in a variety of social issues: the abolition of slavery, health care, accessible education, help for the poor, to name a few. But early in the twentieth century, a division occurred. Fundamentalists feared the erosion of biblical truth that resulted from new liberal teaching. They nailed down the basics of the faith and drew their battle lines. But one of these "new" teachings concerned the Christian's responsibility to reform society. This "social gospel" was really nothing new—Christians had been promoting social justice for centuries—but now the fundamentalists were labeling it "liberal" and holding it with suspicion.

So for most of the middle of the century, fundamentalists (and their evangelical descendants) retreated from social involvement. Our job was to stay holy, to share the truth of Christ, and to worship God. Anyone who talked too much about helping the poor or fighting racism was suspected of leaning leftward. (This is, of course, a generalization. Certainly evangelical Christians were involved in various charities, but there was a strong feeling in the churches that evangelism was all that mattered and that fighting for social justice was a distraction.)

John Perkins began to change that. He had grown up poor in rural Mississippi, one of eight children of sharecropping parents. Realizing that Mississippi was a dead-end for him, he headed for California at age seventeen. Several years later in a California Sunday school he found Christ, and Christ led him back to his home state.

As he began to teach in a church in the town of Mendenhall, Perkins soon realized the needs were more than spiritual. The area was rife with racism. Poverty gripped the black community. There were limited economic opportunities for blacks, and their social options were also slight. Leisure time revolved around several "honky-tonk" bars, and Perkins quickly saw a connection with the problem of teenage pregnancy, which just continued the cycle of poverty. But most of those bars were owned by church members, so when Perkins began teaching about the need for social change, he was asked to stop teaching.

Kicked out of his church, he started his own ministry—Voice of Calvary. This became a model of community development, and not only among Christians. Perkins dared to tackle both the spiritual and social needs of Mendenhall. Voice of Calvary started co-ops, stores, and businesses; built new housing; established jobs; and gave kids some healthy places to hang out. Soon it branched out to other Mississippi communities.

With Justice for All, published in 1982, is Perkins's story and his mission statement. The book is just a part of this man's total influence. Describing the early years of VOC, Perkins writes: "Evangelism was happening! But the realities of daily life in rural Mississippi reminded us constantly of what God had taught us during that first crucial year: evangelism is not enough."

Sounds like the "social gospel," doesn't it? But Perkins had proven his commitment to Jesus Christ—and to evangelism—in his twenty years of ministry. He wasn't just theorizing about what *ought* to be important, he was modeling a ministry that was both evangelistic and transforming, both personal and social. He was following Jesus into a whole-person kind of ministry that the church desperately needed.

Many Christian ministries in urban and rural areas, in the United States and around the world, have adopted and adapted Voice of Calvary's techniques. Many Christian leaders today cite the influence of John Perkins in their lives. And it may be no coincidence that the 1980s saw evangelicals moving back into social involvement, trying to change the world for Jesus Christ.

Worship Is a Verb

1985

ROBERT WEBBER

Worship has hit the big time. Churches everywhere are paying attention to how and why they worship. New styles are adopted, old liturgies reclaimed. Books and magazines debate the details. Church music directors are now called "worship ministers." A whole branch of contemporary Christian music has exploded on the scene: "praise and worship." Many people are choosing a church to attend based on its worship style rather than its preaching.

It wasn't always like this.

Bob Webber likes to tell about one church he visited where the pastor assured him that they'd get "the preliminaries" over quickly so there would be plenty of time to preach. Preliminaries? Well, it's true: For most of the twentieth century, the sermon was the main event in evangelical churches. You went to church to hear the preacher. If you got "blessed" by what the preacher said, you went home happy. All those hymns and prayers and offerings and anthems, well, they were just preliminaries. *Worship* was the Sunday morning service that people sat through. It was very much a noun.

But Christianity has a rich history of *active* worship. Coming out of a Jewish culture in which worshipers raised their hands and danced and made triumphal processions, Christianity adopted many of the same forms. Two millennia of Christian tradition have given us a smorgasbord of musical, dramatic, and liturgical forms to use as we gather to honor our beloved Lord. A Bible professor from Wheaton College, Robert Webber was unearthing these treasures for evangelicals long before anyone else was. He was "worship" before worship was cool.

As an Episcopalian, Webber is more at home with liturgy than most evangelicals. But he boasts a varied résumé, with influences from fundamentalist, charismatic, and evangelical sources.

He understands the importance of "the Word heard"—that is, the preaching—in the evangelical tradition, and he doesn't want to get rid of that. But he also calls for the rediscovery of "the Word enacted" in the Eucharist and in other worship forms. In more recent books, he's been calling for a "blended" worship, which mixes styles of different churches, combining the strong points of the charismatic, liturgical, and free-church traditions.

Many evangelicals don't buy his suggestions. Much of the ancient liturgy still feels like the "vain repetitions" Jesus warned about, especially when mumbled by a church full of day-dreaming parishioners. In the "free" tradition, worshipers like to make it up as they go along. The idea that earlier Christians have given us great words to use, better than those we'd invent on our own—well, that's a hard sell, even for Webber.

But Webber's influence goes beyond the recovery of liturgy. He has challenged a generation of Christians to think about what worship is. Through his books, including the foundational *Common Roots* and the ambitious *Encyclopedia of Christian Worship,* he has awakened churches to the essence of worship. He has taught people that worship *is* a verb, and what a verb! He has inspired people to sing and dance, pray and play, kneel and reel and feel and heal—all because we serve an awesome God. Because of Bob Webber and those who have learned from him, in many churches worship will never again be that stationary, sluggish noun it once was. People are not just attending the worship. They are truly worshiping.

This Present Darkness

1987

FRANK PERETTI

It's hard to believe now, but for most of the twentieth century, evangelical Christians didn't have much taste for fiction. We dealt in matters of truth and doctrine. Our books told true stories of personal testimony or coached us in Christian living. Fiction was trivial, if not downright deceitful.

Then came Frank Peretti. He was a writer, not a preacher or prophet, just a hack who delivered a plot-crackling page-turner about spiritual warfare. *This Present Darkness* took place in a small town in the Pacific Northwest, peopled by ordinary folks named Hank and Kate and fought over by a robust collection of angelic and demonic beings.

It caught something in the Christian consciousness. *We're not just muddling through this suburban existence—we're waging spiritual war.* Politically, culturally, educationally, artistically, evangelicals were primed for battle. The world had been slipping out of our grasp—it was high time to grab it back in God's name. The Reagan Revolution had excited many evangelicals, but many others were realizing the limits of political power. They were ready for Peretti's basic premise: Culture wars are *spiritual.* Victory will be won through prayer, spiritual discipline, and unmasking the ways of the enemy. You can hear it in the songs written for the church in the century's last decade: We have a host of new battle hymns.

In the publishing world *This Present Darkness* was a boulder dropped into a pond. Its publisher, Crossway, was a well-respected but lower-tier company that was edging into fiction. There was little budget for promotion. In fact Peretti's novel was out for about a year before it caught fire, fanned by word of mouth, much of that emanating from pop singer Amy Grant. Then it became a megaseller, spawning Peretti's own sequels as well as a flurry of copycat novels. Suddenly every publisher was scrambling to find Christian fiction. Those that had specialized in theology and Christian living were now looking for plot lines and character development.

You might forgive authors like Janette Oke for wondering what all the excitement was about. She had been quietly selling millions of historical romances in the Christian market throughout the 1980s. There was already a niche carved for her and a handful of successful novelists, with a loyal band of female readers who appreciated the Christian characters and sexual restraint of Oke and her ilk. There was also a substantial market for "biblical fiction"—musings about what the Bible *doesn't* tell us about some of its people.

But Peretti exploded the market for Christian fiction by writing in the present day in an adventure genre. Suddenly it was okay for Christians of any age or gender to read plain old fiction. And publishers raced to supply that need. Before Peretti, your average Christian bookstore might have devoted half a shelf to fiction. Now it's half the store.

Yet the influence of *This Present Darkness* goes far beyond the publishing world. Like many of the important works covered in this book, it capsulized the spirit of its age and propelled it forward. Peretti didn't invent the idea of spiritual warfare but he described it happening in the little town of Ashton. That gave Christians a way of seeing their own towns.

Once a fretful servant accosted the prophet Elisha, pointing to the enemy troops surrounding them. After the prophet prayed, God opened the eyes of the servant so he could see the larger reality, the army of God's angels surrounding the enemy. That was the kind of eye-opening that Peretti gave us. Many of us weren't seeing the enemy; many more weren't seeing the angels. Peretti gave us a way to see the spiritual conflicts of our lives.

The Man in the Mirror

1989

PATRICK M. MORLEY

Through most of the twentieth century, men have been playing hooky from church. Oh, there's always been a cadre of men running the show, but the strength of the rank and file has always been female. Culturally, you can look back at the early { 207 } 1900s to see the church standing up against drinking, smoking, cussing, gambling, and cardplaying—basically the stuff men were doing. "Christian" men had to be genteel and gentle, like the "meek and mild" Jesus the churches kept singing about.

Every so often the church got a shot of testosterone. In the early decades, ex-ballplayer Billy Sunday brought his brawny Christianity into the fight against social ills. In the evangelical resurgence of the 1940s and '50s, there were young bucks like Billy Graham and missionary martyr Jim Elliot who plowed forward for Christ with a youthful exuberance. But these were the exceptions. For most of the century, Christianity has had a feminine flavor. Men might let their wives drag them to church, but you can bet they'd hurry home to watch the ballgame.

In publishing it was the same story. Christian bookstores were frequented by women and pastors, but not the "man in the pew." Publishers would put out theology and Bible study books for church leaders and self-help books and devotionals for church women. Books on "women's issues" (including marriage and family) would sell to women, but no one was really sure what "men's issues" were.

Then came the 1990s. Promise Keepers, led by champion college football coach Bill McCartney, energized thousands on thousands of Christian men. Stadiums were packed with guys cheering, not for their favorite teams but for *Jesus!* "I love Jesus, yes I do! I love Jesus, how 'bout you?" Speakers challenged men to keep their promises to God, to their wives and children, to their churches, to their pastors. Guys were hugging in the aisles and even weeping openly, but no one would tease them for these emotional displays. Suddenly it was manly to follow Christ.

Patrick Morley's book, *The Man in the Mirror,* was foundational for the modern men's movement. Predating Promise Keepers, it sparked a wave of books for Christian men that's still going strong. Morley, a successful businessman and a Bible teacher in Florida, concisely defined "men's issues." The book bore the tag line: "Solving the 24 problems men face." And there they were— identity, purpose, relationships, money, decisions, anger, independence, integrity, and sixteen more. *The Man in the Mirror* succeeded not so much with new ideas but with straight talk about issues no one had been talking much about.

Recent studies of gender differences have shown us how men tend to compartmentalize their lives. They easily wall off their faith from, say, their business lives or their relationships. That explains why men could do the church thing on Sunday and be ruthless, conniving wheeler-dealers at work on Monday. Their faith was real; it just stayed in its place. It didn't have much effect on the rest of their lives.

But Morley's book issued a firm challenge to Christian men to live what they believed. The Promise Keepers movement and a shelf of later books continued with that challenge. How does a Christian man manage money, for instance? How does a Christian man develop a friendship? How does a Christian man make decisions? How does a Christian man treat his wife? These questions had been covered before in various publications, which were seldom seen by the men in the pews (and those home watching the game). Morley packed it all into one hard-hitting book that made men start to pay attention.

Experiencing God

1990

HENRY T. BLACKABY
and CLAUDE V. KING

Occasionally a new book surprises the publishing world. Some upstart company puts out a best-seller, or perhaps it's self-published. There's no great budget behind the book's suc- cess—no TV ads, store displays, talk show appearances. The book succeeds through word of mouth because it meets a need. And the executives in the major publishing houses are left shaking their heads, wondering, *Why didn't we see that coming?* (And they scramble to produce their own books to meet the newly recognized need.)

The modern craze for Christian fiction started that way, when Peretti's *This Present Darkness* struck gold. In the last few years of the century, we've seen another low-key book gain popularity: *Experiencing God* by Blackaby and King. Church Bible studies are using it as a curriculum and passing it throughout their churches, and to other churches. The Southern Baptist Convention was the incubator for this book (Blackaby and King both work with the SBC), but *Experiencing God* has crossed many denominational borders. (We have seen it used broadly in our Methodist and Presbyterian churches.)

What's the appeal? *Experiencing God* covers a subject that (amazingly) keeps getting lost in our ecclesiastical shuffles. We all want to experience God, don't we? But how quickly we forget about that as we hurry from our potluck suppers to our protest marches. Some churches emphasize knowledge *about* God and about the Bible. Some want to fight *for* God and redeem our society. Some want to draw new believers *toward* God and communicate effectively with seekers. There's nothing wrong with any of that, except it all leaves us hungering for something more basic: experiencing God's presence in our lives. That's the hunger that Blackaby and King have addressed.

Critics have panned the book for several reasons. Sure, it's simplistic and it uses too many stories about church buildings and ministries and finances. But somehow its readers have been getting past all those problems. They've been learning how to experience God in their own lives—and in their own churches.

Experiencing God is systematic and practical, offering seven principles and ways of applying them. "God is always at work around you" is the first principle. Blackaby and King go on to talk about how God invites us to work with him, how he speaks to us, and how we can respond to him. If God has seemed merely like an academic notion to you, or some distant spiritual entity, this is exciting stuff—you can participate in the work of God! And if your church has too many committee meetings and not enough life-changing events, these ideas are revolutionary.

The book is actually a workbook with assignments for twelve "units" of five days each. Readers are led in the study of Scripture and invited to write down their responses. Publishers will tell you that workbooks don't sell, that no one wants to go back to school. Guess again. Often a book will be so successful that a workbook will be published later. In this case the workbook came first (1990), and the book with the same title followed (1994); both achieved best-seller status.

We know it's iffy to put such a recent book in our list of the most important Christian books of the century. Usually you need time to sift out the trivial from the tried and true. But we include *Experiencing God* not only on its own merits, but as a representative of all the "little" books that bring Christian publishing back to its basic principles—authors with ideas to share with readers, ideas that just might change some lives.

Disappointment with God

1990

PHILIP YANCEY

We Christians have always been great at denial. Oh, we go through our dark nights of the soul, doubting God and struggling with sin, but we don't talk about these times very much. We put on our best Christian face for the other Christians we know and we all pretend everything's fine.

Then along comes a writer like Philip Yancey to tear down our pretenses. Yancey is the junior high kid in the back of your Sunday school class who keeps raising his hand when you're trying to shush everyone by quoting Romans 8:28. "Yeah, that sounds good, but what about . . . ?" He just won't let you off the hook.

Maybe that comes from his stint as writer and editor for *Campus Life* magazine in the turbulent '70s. That generation of high school readers was questioning everything their parents taught them. Later Yancey began writing a column for *Christianity Today,* giving an adult audience the benefit of his soul-searching. Along the way, he has put out a handful of books that grapple honestly with tough questions: *Where Is God When It Hurts?* (with Dr. Paul Brand); *Disappointment with God; The Jesus I Never Knew;* and *What's So Amazing about Grace?* Again and again he sidesteps the easy answers and raises issues we've tried to avoid.

Disappointment with God weaves a discussion of the book of Job around several modern examples of human suffering. It's the age-old problem of evil, addressed with sensitivity and wisdom. Why do the righteous suffer? Why doesn't God protect us the way we want? What should we do when we feel God has let us down?

Yancey's no cutting-edge philosopher. He doesn't arrive at any startling new answers—but that's sort of the point. He dares to point out that, after thirty-some chapters of Job's gut-wrenching questions, God finally speaks . . . but even God doesn't answer the questions. Yet there is great value in listening for God's voice, wrestling with the angels, calling fire from heaven—even if we don't always get what we want. Yancey gives us permission to ask the questions, and his sweet prose guides us as we admit that we too have sometimes been disappointed by the God we love.

All the books in Yancey's arsenal are like this: bold in their questions, amazingly orthodox in their answers. He has gained a following among Christians in general, but especially among *hurting* Christians, those who have struggled with disease, divorce, doubt, or depression. He has given a voice to those on the fringes of the church.

In his later books, *The Jesus I Never Knew* and *What's So Amazing About Grace?*, Yancey calls Christians to be what they are—followers of Jesus, saved by God's grace. He challenges some false notions of Jesus and theology that have put down deep roots in our churches. In his unassuming manner, Yancey leads readers along a path of discovery—rediscovery. Here, look at the Jesus I found! Hey, what's this grace thing all about? And how can we be so judgmental when (a) we serve a Jesus who loved people deeply, and (b) we recognize that we as sinners are wholly dependent on God's grace? Again, Yancey isn't charting a brand-new course, just asking the questions and steering us toward the God of the Scriptures.

Left Behind

1995

TIM LaHAYE
and JERRY B. JENKINS

What do an airline pilot, a magazine reporter, a college student, the Romanian president, a beautiful flight attendant, and the visitation pastor of a church have in common? In the mega-selling novel of the late 1990s, when the rapture whisks millions of Christians away, these characters are among the millions more who are *left behind.*

The plot is a familiar one to pre-trib students of the endtimes. We've seen it in Scofield's notes, the old *Thief in the Night* movie, *The Late Great Planet Earth,* and Larry Norman's classic song "I Wish We'd All Been Ready." When believers are caught up to "meet him in the air," what happens to all the other people on earth?

According to *Left Behind,* the mass disappearance causes chaos in society, as people struggle to explain it. Aliens? A new kind of nuclear weapon? Of course some people realize (too late) that this was the rapture predicted in the Bible. The confusion leaves the door open for a charismatic young leader from a European country who seems too good to be true. A few of the new believers suspect that he's the Antichrist of biblical prophecy. This novel and its several sequels map out a course of events that fit the pretribulation view of biblical prophecy—the rapture followed by seven years of tribulation, during which the Antichrist emerges and the nations of earth rise up against the Lord, culminating in the battle of Armageddon.

Of course there are other interpretations of Scripture. Some Christians are "posttribulational" or "midtrib" or even "amillennial" in their beliefs about Christ's return. But the pre-trib view has been especially robust in the twentieth century, popularized by C. I. Scofield, the Moody empire, and Hal Lindsey, among others. And whatever your beliefs, you have to admit that this view makes a great story.

That's what LaHaye and Jenkins capitalize on. LaHaye, a Bible teacher, has long had a feel for the conservative Christian audience. His *Spirit-Controlled Temperament* predated the Christian counseling movement with a simple method of self-understanding. (Long before Myers and Briggs labeled us with letters—INFP, ESTJ—LaHaye was asking whether we were melancholic or phlegmatic.) Jenkins, a former editor of *Moody* magazine, is perhaps the most prolific writer on the evangelical scene, with more than a hundred books to his credit. These two authors combined their talents to produce a publishing juggernaut.

By the end of the century, *Left Behind* had sold several million copies, and the entire series had sold more than ten million copies. Secular best-seller lists have long been skewed against books sold in Christian stores, but they couldn't ignore the numbers coming from the LaHaye-Jenkins series.

Maybe it's the new millennium. Maybe the Y2K bug got people worried about the end of civilization. Since the 1960s, Christians have been crowing about the world's downhill slide (a key element in the pretribulation plot). Israel's growth as a nation (another key element) has added to the drama. And certain aspects of modern life (satellite TV, bar codes, computer-driven commerce) have made parts of this vision eerily real. Stir in some computer hysteria and the end-of-the-world hype that accompanies every new millennium (well, it happened in 1000 A.D.), and people are going to be interested in endtimes prophecy.

All of this, no doubt, has fueled the success of the *Left Behind* books, and those books have returned the favor, fueling this new endtimes interest in the church and in society at large.

The Purpose-Driven Church

1995

RICK WARREN

For most of the twentieth century, evangelical churches tried very hard to keep new people out. Oh, they didn't know they were doing this. In fact most leaders of these churches were probably wringing their hands, wondering why no one new was showing up. But nearly everything these churches did in their services was sending the signal: Keep out!

One of the major church trends of the last two decades has been the new attention paid to "seekers"—people who are considering a relationship with God but are not yet committed. Willow Creek Community Church in Illinois has become the largest church in the United States by wooing such people. Using somewhat different tactics, Rick Warren has had similar success with his Saddleback Community Church in Southern California. Seeing these success stories, many other churches have tried to copy these methods, with mixed results.

The key to these successful churches is not necessarily their methods, but their *intentionality*. Willow Creek and Saddleback decided what they wanted to do and then figured out the best way to do it. Common sense, right? But it's amazing how seldom most churches have thought about what they really intend to do.

And that's where Rick Warren's book offers help. Telling the story of his own church and its growth, Warren shows churches how to be purpose-driven. "The issue is church health," he says, "not church growth. If your church is healthy, growth will occur naturally. Healthy consistent growth is the result of balancing the five biblical purposes of the church."

In 1980 Rick Warren graduated from seminary in Fort Worth, Texas, and moved with his wife to Southern California, to begin a church in the living room of their home in the Saddleback Valley of Orange County. The church began with the Warrens and one other family, but it soon became the fastest-growing Baptist church in the history of America, and at the time the book was written it was averaging more than ten thousand in attendance. Warren was committed to the idea that if his church was to grow, it should grow by "conversion growth," not from "transfer growth." For its first fifteen years, it didn't have a building, but that didn't stop its growth. At various times some seventy-nine different facilities were used to house the growing congregation.

The five-part strategy that Warren propounds is that a church should seek to grow: (1) warmer through fellowship, (2) deeper through discipleship, (3) stronger through worship, (4) broader through ministry, and (5) larger through evangelism.

The Purpose-Driven Church capsulizes the latest shift in church strategy. In the first half of the century, very little was written about the art of running a church. Much was said about fundamentalism and modernism, and seminaries taught theology and homiletics, but church growth was not a hot topic. A church just *was*. Why bother to define its purpose?

As the evangelical movement began to flower midcentury, there was a lot of talk about evangelism, but this was done mostly in individual conversations outside the church, in stadiums by famous evangelists, or in churches filled with people who were already Christians. Some began to see evangelism as at least one of the church's purposes, but how could a church connect with unbelievers?

Still, some experts were beginning to consider how churches could bring new people in. Lyle Schaller, a city planner turned Methodist minister, started writing books on church management. Church growth analysts (Donald McGavran, Peter Wagner, Win Arn, and others) turned their efforts from the mission field to U.S. churches. Pollster George Barna began analyzing the church's work in marketing terms.

Many Christians balked at the businesslike quality of all this. Some refused to define success in terms of numbers. Frankly, many small churches *liked* being small. And a number of church leaders still have questions about how the church growth movement and the seeker-oriented churches are *defining* the church.

But Rick Warren's book throws down a gauntlet to any church leader. (Lyle Schaller, who may have started the plethora of books on church growth and management, called it "the best book I've ever read on how to do church in today's world.") What is your purpose? Why do you do what you do? What should you be doing? How will you do that? These are the questions that, when answered, will propel local churches well into the twenty-first century.

The Runners-Up

No doubt, you are surprised at some of the books that didn't make the list. At times we wished we could expand the list to 150; but probably when we got to 150, we would have wanted to add 50 more.

If this were a list of the *best* Christian books, you might see the works of outstanding writers like Flannery O'Connor, T. S. Eliot, Annie Dillard, J. R. R. Tolkien, and Walter Wangerin. They certainly would deserve to be on a list of *best* books.

And if this were a list of the outstanding theological works of the century that influenced ministers and seminarians, we would have included works by Albert Schweitzer, John A. T. Robinson, Louis Berkhof, Martin Buber, Cornelius Van Til, Benjamin Warfield, Gerhard Kittel, George Ladd, and Edward John Carnell.

If this were a list of the evangelical best-sellers of the century, we certainly would have included books by Charlie Shedd, Kevin Leman, Gary Smalley, Charles Swindoll, Brother Andrew, Willard Harley, Janette Oke, and John MacArthur. They all had worthy books, and books that sold into the hundreds of thousands, if not millions, of copies.

Then there were other books that came within an eyelash of making it, but because we got up on the wrong side of bed that day (or because we felt we had enough already from that decade), we chose not to include them.

Here are some of them:

The Frog in the Kettle by George Barna
The Christian Mind by Harry Blamires
How to Manage Your Money by Larry Burkett
The Christian Family by Larry Christenson
The Pattern of God's Truth by Frank Gaebelein
Joshua by Joseph F. Girzone
Hind's Feet on High Places by Hannah Hurnard
A Shepherd Looks at Psalm 23 by Philip Keller
A Testament of Devotion by Thomas Kelly
Dare to Live Now by Bruce Larson

The History of the Expansion of Christianity by Kenneth Scott Latourette

Ordering Your Private World by Gordon MacDonald

Healing by Francis McNutt

Inasmuch by David Moberg

Jesus Rediscovered by Malcolm Muggeridge

The Normal Christian Life by Watchman Nee

The Scandal of the Evangelical Mind by Mark Noll

Hudson Taylor and Maria by J. C. Pollock

The Universe Next Door by James Sire

The Person and Work of the Holy Spirit by R. A. Torrey

Intended for Pleasure by Ed Wheat

In addition, there are dozens of books by personal friends that probably belonged on the list and who probably will never forgive us because they aren't; to them we apologize for the oversight, and promise that next century we will do better.

Index of Names

{ 221 }

{ 222 }

William J. Petersen began reviewing books for Christian magazines in 1950. In 1955 he developed *Christian Bookseller* magazine, the first magazine for the Christian bookselling industry, and became its first editorial director. In 1958, as executive editor of *Eternity* magazine, he launched the first Christian Book-of-the-Year contest, polling experts across the country to determine the top twenty-five Christian books of the year. In 1997 he became the first recipient of the Joseph T. Bayly Award "for outstanding service to Chrisian periodical publishing," presented by the Evangelical Press Association.

Petersen has written more than twenty books on various subjects, including biography, Bible study, cults, hymnology, and travel. He and his wife, Ardythe, are the parents of three grown children and live in Pennsylvania, where he continues to serve as senior editor of Fleming H. Revell.

Randy Petersen has written thirty books on various themes, including church history, psychology, Bible study, devotionals, puzzles, sports, and fiction. He formerly served on the staff of *Eternity* magazine as editor of *Evangelical Newsletter* and the *Bible Newsletter*. Active in his Methodist church in New Jersey, Randy also acts, directs, and teaches in local theaters and schools.